SURVIVING AND THRIVING IN MINISTRY

Lessons I Learned; Mistakes I Made

Dr. Justin W. Tull

Copyright 2013

Surviving and Thriving in Ministry
Copyright 2013 © Justin W Tull
All rights Reserved

No part of this book may be reproduced or transmitted in any form or by any means, electronic or mechanical, including photocopying and recording or by any information storage or retrieval system.

Cover photo of Oak Lawn UMC, Dallas, Texas, by John Lovelace
Cover and interior design by Sidewalk Labs.

Requests for permission should be addressed to
justinwtull@yahoo.com

ISBN: 1489566996
ISBN-13: 978-1489566997

Scripture Quotations, unless otherwise indicated, are from New Revised Standard Version Bible, Copyright 1989
National Council of the Churches of Christ in the United States of America.
Used by permission. All rights reserved.

This book is dedicated to the eleven churches
I was privileged to serve.
These communities of faith taught me lessons in
God's amazing grace.

CONTENTS

INTRODUCTION	**1**

SURVIVING MINISTRY:

AN IMPERFECT CHURCH	**4**
People in the church don't always act Christian!	4
Never let pious ones intimidate!	9
Don't allow complainers and critics to get to you!	14
SPIRITUAL MANDATES FOR SURVIVAL	**19**
Forgive your enemies!	19
Let go of resentment from past irritations!	24

THRIVING IN MINISTRY:

FINDING FIRM FOUNDATIONS	**30**
God empowers ministry!	30
Develop strong friendships within the clergy family!	36
Allow the saints to cheer you on!	42
LEADERSHIP MANDATES	**47**
Don't make unilateral decisions!	47
Dare to be a manager!	51
Resist the temptation to over-manage!	57
Build a team!	61
Stay connected to enemies and leadership!	65
SELF CARE ESSENTIALS	**71**
Accept the fact that you will never get it all done!	71
Care for the whole self…mind, body, and soul!	75
Develop spiritual disciplines!	78
Work at working out!	82
Recognize when help is needed!	87
SHARPENING SKILLS AND STRATEGIES	**90**
Take time to plan sermons long-term!	90
Dare to preach without a net!	94
Be a leader in stewardship!	97
Adopt a less-anxious presence!	102
RESPONDING TO GOD'S CALL	**107**
Looking back with thanks!	107
Surviving or Thriving?	111

INTRODUCTION

Decades ago when I was in seminary I was privileged to read Reinhold Niebuhr's classic, *Leaves from the Notebook of a Tamed Cynic*. I gained much practical advice as he shared honestly his struggles during his early days of ministry. Remembering his words of warning, wisdom and encouragement, I was able to avoid several mistakes as I began my own ministerial journey. Along the way, I would learn my own lessons through both positive and negative experiences. Throughout my ministry, I have become painfully aware of the difficulty that ministers have in surviving the pressures, temptations, and burdens that come with the job. However, despite the fact that ministry is laced with these negative impediments, it is also amply supplied with experiences of deep meaning and purpose. This book is an effort to share some strategies for staying healthy in body, mind, and spirit and to offer a collegial warning concerning needless pitfalls along the way. Hopefully, through insights gained in one's own ministry and from lessons gleaned from the pages of this book, ministers will do more than simply *survive* ministry; they will *thrive*.

In sharing both my mistakes and insights, I decided to take a rather presumptuous step—to assume that my experience and conclusions were not only pertinent to me but would also prove to be "on target" for other clergy. Therefore, I have offered my insights and conclusions as simple imperatives, trusting the reader to discern the validity of each bit of pastoral advice. If I can spare a few ministers some of my own mistakes, if I can help some pastors gain positive habits and behavior far quicker than I was able to manage, then this project will be well worth the effort. I, for one, am not content with ministerial survival. If we are to be truly effective pastors, we must learn to deal positively with the pressures, dangers, and distractions that could rob us of effectiveness and a sense of well-being. Here's hoping that all those who accept the call to ministry will find in its sacred office a vocation that is both fruitful and fulfilling!

Surviving Ministry

CHAPTER ONE

AN IMPERFECT CHURCH

PEOPLE IN THE CHURCH DON'T ALWAYS ACT CHRISTIAN
Church members are imperfect, just like their pastor.

In my sixth year of ministry I was finally in a church large enough to have a part-time secretary. After a church break-in, the secretary felt unsafe and resigned. I had the job of interviewing candidates for her replacement. One applicant had only average qualifications but I decided to interview her anyway. During the interview I asked her why she wanted to work for the church. Her response startled me. "I just want to work in a place where people are Christian and you are surrounded with love!" Needless to say, she did not get the job. If we had hired her, I would have had a long talk with her about her expectations of church life. I would have warned her that people in the church don't always act Christian.

Some pastors begin ministry expecting the behavior of their congregation to be a slight cut above those outside the church. Newly appointed ministers already know from their previous church experience that many members will fail to be mature Christians. But what they may not expect is that a surprising number of members are power-hungry and others are downright mean-spirited. Ironically, many of these destructive types falsely believe that they are working in the church's best interest. Because church members often see confrontation as an unacceptable behavior, these negative power brokers can often get their way and, in extreme cases, even hold the church hostage. It did not take me long to discover that the church has an ample supply of people who are petty and still others who are ready to unleash their deep-seated anger if they are not held in check. The difference in perception between a church member and a pastor is often that the pastor sees the totality of these negative forces while most church members see only those in their immediate circles. How a pastor deals with this ugly underbelly of the church is of utmost importance to his or her ministerial effectiveness and state of mind. Sometimes pastoral intervention is required to make certain that these destructive persons have limited power and influence. But in dealing with most of the "work in progress" Christians, a much more tolerant and loving response is needed.

In one church a couple set up a conference with me to air their concerns. I knew they had been unhappy with the church for some time. They also did not seem overly fond of me or my preaching. But at the heart of their dissatisfaction was their conviction that the church was not spiritual enough. It seemed to me that their attitude was more angry than disappointed, more judgmental than compassionate. They expressed frustration over being surrounded by people who did not take the church as seriously as they did. They wanted members of the church to be more Christian, which I interpreted as being more like them. After a lengthy visit with me, they soon left our church and joined another church in the area.

During the conference with these disgruntled members, I remember thinking to myself that I also was dissatisfied with the behavior and level of commitment of many of the members.

An Imperfect Church

I agreed that many members were not as "Christian" as they should be. But I did not share the couple's strong disdain for those they considered "slackers of the faith." I did not feel a swell of righteous indignation against members who failed to live up to the demanding qualities of the Christian life—integrity, fidelity, compassion, graciousness, and love. Indeed, I thought that part of my job as pastor was to help everyone in the church, including myself, grow in faith and faithfulness. I did not expect to find everyone to be at the same place in their spiritual journey. Indeed, some in our church might have even resembled the "prodigal."

So, what is a pastor supposed to do with the pettiness and meanness in the church—ignore it or simply condemn it? No, the pastor is to stand against the misrepresentations of the faith and the distortions of Christian living, but not with a stone in the hand or a scowl on the face, as if we, the clergy, are without fault. The pastor's role is to preach, teach, and demonstrate a life of love and faith, where mistakes are made but forgiveness is given—a life where drawing a line between good and bad people is always counterproductive.

I imagine that Jesus must have felt disappointed many times when his disciples failed to measure up. They were petty, jealous, self-absorbed, fearful, ignorant, dense—to name only a few of their weaknesses. And Jesus reacted to their behavior in a variety of ways—patience, judgment, reassurance, disappointment, compassion, and encouragement. But he never hated them or treated them with total disdain. More importantly, he never gave up on them. Even when they showed little signs of improvement, even when they seemed to be clueless as to their mission, Jesus continued to entrust them with the keys to the kingdom. With all of their limitations, this motley crew was his team and he was sticking with them.

Instead of washing his hands of the whole group, he washed their feet.

As a pastor of thirty-eight years, I understand all too well the imperfections of the church and the fickleness of church members, but I still choose to work with the entire congregation committed to my care—they are still the main team. I believe that there is a potential faithful disciple in every last one of the church's flawed members. But what keeps me going, keeps me positive in my efforts, is that scattered throughout the imperfect church are also the gracious saints who are a powerful reminder that the church remains in the transformation business. These saints exhibit what the Christian life should be; they define discipleship. So what better candidates for transformation can there be than the petty and the mean, the apathetic and self-absorbed, the troublemaker and the prodigal? Jesus worked with such as these and through their ministry the world was turned right side up.

I still don't like to see pettiness and meanness in the church, but I don't lose heart. Who knows? Maybe there is hope even for a less-than-perfect pastor.

An Imperfect Church

QUESTIONS FOR REFLECTION

- In what way has the "unchristian" behavior of church members ever surprised you or made you angry?

- Do you ever feel contempt for those who do not behave in a Christian way? How do you resolve such feelings?

- When is it appropriate to stand up against church members who are bringing harm to others in the church? What strategies do you use to oppose them?

Never Let Pious Ones Intimidate!
*There will always be those more spiritual,
just not the ones who claim to be.*

It was early in my ministry when I discovered a group of youth in my church who were more spiritual than I was. It was disarming. I was the one called by God to be a minister. I had spent four years in seminary. I was to be the spiritual leader of the church and yet these adolescents were praying circles around me. They read their Bibles daily. They witnessed their faith to their friends and even to strangers. My first impression of these devoted youth was that they were incredibly mature Christians.

Ironically, their extraordinary pious behavior did not spark in me a desire to deepen my own spiritual life. Rather, their apparent devotion just made me feel guilty and raised questions about my own spirituality. I did my best to relate to these youth as their pastor. Gradually I was able to accept the idea that despite their age, these young people were better Christians, or at least more religious than I was.

It was well into the second year of my appointment that a clear revelation came to me as I led a youth canoe trip. For various reasons, including the curse of Murphy's Law, the trip that I had promoted as fun and leisurely had become, after a last minute change of plans, a grueling affair. To reach our destination of 31 miles downstream we had to travel about 14 water miles a day. We had youth as young as thirteen and as old as eighteen, plus the adult leaders. Fortunately, I knew I could count on the older ones of the youth group who were strong bodied and also my most devoted Christians. They would provide the strong leadership I needed.

On the last night of the trip—a very hard day—we arrived at our campsite around six in the evening. We were all exhausted. As soon as my foot hit the rocky beach I requested everyone's help in setting up the tents, beginning meal preparation, and unloading the canoes. Many, despite their aches and blisters, sprang into action knowing that there was much to be done. But one group of youth began complaining how hard the trip was and how it was not like it was promoted. For about an hour they sat on their duffle bags complaining and doing nothing. I was too busy getting the meal ready to make a second plea for help, but I made a mental note of this group's childish behavior.

When the time came for the devotional, I decided to change my message. I must admit that as I spoke to those around the campfire, my tone was a bit accusatory. My devotional was not a complete "Woe to you" rant, but it certainly had all the markings of strong Christian admonition. I told the group that the Christian life was not just about reading the Bible, praying, and acting religious, but also about pitching in, being considerate, and "doing to others as we would have them do unto us." The big surprise of the evening was that I was directing my remarks and my eye contact upon a most unlikely group--not the rambunctious, immature seventh and eighth graders—but the spiritual A Team, the ones best at praying, reading the Bible, and giving testimonies! For the first time I saw this group in a completely different light—not as "witnesses of the Word," but as those who failed to be "doers of the Word." Their behavior had indeed been the worst of the entire group.

These older youth did seem to be convicted of their wrong and for the remainder of the trip volunteered anytime help was requested. Embarrassingly, I was not excited over their improved behavior. Instead, I took some delight in knowing that they were not the mature Christians they professed to be. During the rest of my tenure I was no longer intimidated by them, which was a welcome relief. I also began to understand that true spirituality must always bear fruit in the form of Christ-like behavior. This notion was not unknown to me, but I had not fully taken it into account as I assessed individual spirituality. I certainly was aware of Jesus' words about having to bear good fruit. I knew well the words from James that I had memorized in the junior department of Sunday school: "Be doers of the word and not hearers only." But now I was able to incorporate these elements into my world of feelings and personal interaction. Before the canoe trip I had never understood spirituality in its fullest sense. Now I got it: spirit and action must go together. Spirituality becomes weak without bodily exercise.

My lesson in spirituality would gain an even deeper meaning much later in my ministry. The realization was gradual instead of being sparked by one event or by only one saintly church member. But this insight into spirituality induced a feeling far better than the one I experienced on the canoe trip— rejoicing in catching someone falling short and thereby feeling better about oneself. It finally became apparent to me that even though I was the minister of the church, I did not have to be the best Christian in the church. In fact, I am not sure I could have ever claimed that title in any of the churches I served. In most of my churches I could easily point to countless persons who should be invited into the kingdom ahead of me. I am convinced that God did not call me into ministry because he knew I could be the "number one saint" in the churches I would serve. Rather, he called me to preach the Word and to love the people, all the while knowing that many of my flock would exhibit a greater capacity for living out the gospel. What a relief to know that I did not have to be the lone guru of spirituality. I could delight in rubbing shoulders with all the saints. They could inspire me instead of intimidating me. But as

An Imperfect Church

for those who might claim to be the most spiritual, I now know they are the "least likely" candidates for the honor. Since those early years of ministry, I would no longer be impressed or intimidated by pseudo spirituality, nor would it produce in me self disdain. I still remember those days when I foolishly thought spirituality was a competition. Now I know better.

QUESTIONS FOR REFLECTION

- Do you believe as an ordained clergy that you are supposed to be the "best Christian" in the church?

- What are the most helpful spiritual disciplines in your daily life? What area of your spiritual life would you like to improve?

- Are you able to affirm both privately and publically the spiritual maturity of the saints of your church? Do you allow them to inspire you rather than intimidate you?

Don't Allow Complainers and Critics to Get to You!
*Don't take it personally or too seriously.
It's more about them than you!*

Many people might assume that the most difficult part of ministry is dealing with so many serious issues: tragedy, sickness, grief and matters of life and death. Pastors themselves may list the countless meetings, long hours, and the awesome responsibility of preaching and running a church as why ministry is so stressful and draining. All of these aspects of the job certainly add to clergy stress, but perhaps nothing has weighed heavier in my ministry than petty complaints and unwarranted criticism. The serious parts of ministry at least have their rewards and offer a sense of meaning and purpose. Dealing with criticism and pettiness, however, can often end in resentment and even depression. At one time in my ministry my inner child, my sense of playfulness, was at risk because of a barrage of criticism and petty complaints. So oppressive was this negative feedback, even when from well-meaning members, that I finally told my wife, my best and most diplomatic critic, to withhold any criticism about my ministerial performance. I had reached my critical comment limit.

What has been especially painful about criticism and petty complaints during my ministry is that I have experienced it in the midst of being extremely conscientious in all my ministerial roles. Had I been sloppy in the discharge of my duties or devoid of gifts and graces, such negative feedback would have at least been justified.

Through the years I have made several mistakes in responding to criticism whether it was the fair or unwarranted variety. Early on, I paid too much attention to both kinds of critical feedback. Rather than brushing off the absurd comments, I allowed them to evolve from irritation into full-blown resentment. When more serious and valid criticisms came my way I made a second mistake in handling negative feedback. At first this new approach seemed to be a more mature response, but it would eventually lead to collateral damage both for me and the church. After failing to handle criticism with resistance and resentment, I tried responding to criticism by becoming a "conscientious improver." If the criticism had some merit I would concentrate on making improvement in that area. Surprisingly this approach actually resulted in some significant improvement in my pastoral productivity. What I later learned, however, was that my "improvements" were never to be acknowledged by my critics. Gradually I began to understand that when one caters to critics by improving the area of "weakness," the self-appointed critic just identifies another shortcoming to take its place.

I think clergy would be wise, in dealing with criticism, to always suspect that "the issue" in criticism may not be the real issue at all. One danger in catering to the criticisms of others is that one can pursue that issue when another avenue is far more important. In one church I was so busy "improving" my weaknesses and trying to follow the role set by previous pastors that I failed to fully engage my unique strengths and abilities. In so doing I neglected to discern what was most needed for the church at that time in its history. In retrospect, I should have helped the church to define its identity apart from its former pastors and to formulate a clear vision of its future. My "conscientious improver" tactic turned out to be flawed and in the end just fostered a resentment toward my critics and indirectly to the church at large.

In my recent years of retirement, I have become involved in interim ministry. In the training I learned a new mantra for dealing with criticism. I could have used this mantra to my advantage during my early days of ministry. The

An Imperfect Church

imperative is cleverly named "Q tips" which stands for "Quit taking it personally, stupid!" Had I heeded well this mantra throughout my ministry I would have avoided much frustration and resentment. In the process of my ministry I have gradually learned to handle criticism in a more positive manner. Part of the improvement was due to better understanding human nature and accepting the fact that criticism often says more about the critic than the one being criticized. I have also come to expect unresolved anger being directed at clergy. The real source may be anger stemming from unresolved grief or guilt, or problems at work or home. In times of conflict or high anxiety within the church, I now expect to receive either harsh words or harsh criticism from someone who is being overcome with anxiety. In such circumstances, I tell myself the anger is not about me.

Perhaps my most helpful insight concerning criticism came from Lewis Smedes who introduced me to a text from Philippians that provides an antidote to criticism. In his book, *How Can Everything Be All Right When Everything Is all Wrong?*, Smedes chose 1 Corinthians 4:3-4 as the text for the chapter entitled: "All the World's a Critic, and You're Tired of Reading the Reviews." The words from Corinthians have given me a "big picture" perspective in dealing with harsh criticisms that threaten to undo me. Paul, who has his own struggles with criticism, writes, "With me it is a very small thing that I should be judged by you or by any human court. I do not even judge myself…It is the Lord who judges me (1 Cor. 4:3-5)." This text has come to my mind on many occasions and offered me both comfort and courage. Perhaps every pastor's study should have a framed copy of this text hanging on the wall. And if there is space, a large poster could also proclaim its mantra: "It's not about me!" To complete the proper ministerial décor, a glass jar filled with Q tips could be placed on the desk, bringing to mind its own helpful slogan: "Quit taking it personally, stupid!"

I wish I could say that during my ministry I totally mastered dealing with criticism and petty complaints—such is not the case. However, I have made great progress in handling negative remarks. In more recent years such criticism has neither unhinged me nor produced deep-seated resentment. My big regret is that I did not develop such skills much earlier in my ministry. I know now that there is no need for any minister to try to please the most persistent critic or strive for a ninety-five percent approval rating. No biblical character, president or pastor has ever approached those numbers. To strive for such approval would put one in jeopardy of abandoning the calling, and setting oneself up for both disappointment and resentment. I have learned that it is better to be concerned about what God thinks of me and what I think about myself than to worry about other's "opinions" of me. In dealing with the darts of criticism, it is not thicker skin we need; we need a wiser heart.

QUESTIONS FOR REFLECTION

- What experience of the church creates in you a strong sense of vulnerability?

- What angers you the most about life in the church?

- Has criticism ever created in you a buildup of resentment?

- Have you ever been a "conscientious improver"? Have you ever resented critics who are never appeased? If so, who ultimately caused such resentment—the critic or the one who "aimed to please"?

CHAPTER TWO

SPIRITUAL MANDATES FOR SURVIVAL

FORGIVE YOUR ENEMIES!
It is a commandment to both preach and practice!

Some questions about the Bible are difficult, but one question is a no brainer: "What is the most difficult teaching of Jesus?" Do you have it yet? It's loving our enemies and praying for those who hurt us. I cannot think of anything more difficult than that. As preachers we are required to proclaim this central commandment to our people. As Christian ministers we are commanded to follow its imperative ourselves.

For two decades in ministry no church member made this commandment an extreme test for me. Yes, several members did some tacky things to me. I had a few who spread false rumors. None of these actions seriously threatened my future or my basic well-being. But when my difficult challenge finally came, I would realize the extreme difficulty of Jesus' command: I was to forgive those who challenged my worth as a pastor. How does one respond to that? What does one do with that anger?

The details of the event are unimportant for the reader. All you need to know is that I was betrayed by a small faction within the church even though at the time it felt like the whole

Spiritual Mandates for Survival

church. The "event" was so traumatic that I quickly made a drastic decision—I would make an official request to be moved at the next appointment time, some six months away. Instinctively I knew my physical and mental survival depended on it. It was not the first attack from these few, but I decided it would be their last.

After my decision to request a move I had another challenge: "How would I survive spiritually?" My Christian mandate was so simple and yet so difficult: I had to forgive all those who tried to force me to move. My first spiritual test would come very quickly. After reading to the Staff Parrish Relations Committee my letter declaring both my intent to move and the specific reasons for doing so, I was asked to close the meeting with prayer. I had just bared my soul—I was still bleeding from an open wound—and the chair asked me to close that emotionally laden meeting with prayer. Somehow God empowered me to pray a prayer of reconciliation instead a prayer of righteous indignation.

During the weeks that followed I knew that I had to rid myself of the anger and hurt if I were to continue my life as a minister. I also knew I had to let go of this hurt even if I were to leave the profession. I sought the help of a counselor to sort out my feelings and to begin my healing process. I leaned heavily upon my wife for her comfort and support. She was a rock.

What I soon discovered was that "Forgiveness" with the capital 'F' was not something that could be accomplished instantaneously but only in a cyclical process—two steps forward, one step back. After my surprisingly gracious prayer at the meeting, I soon found myself becoming more and more angry. I called one of the perpetrators and told him why I found his actions grossly unfair and misguided. He continued to defend his tactics as being motivated for the good of the church.

I cannot recall how long it took for me to let go of the anger. But during my angriest moments I never hated any of the people who had wronged me. I certainly did not like them but I did not wish them harm. What I wanted most from them was true contrition, which never came. The recurring test of forgiveness came each time I would see them. Sometimes when I thought the process of forgiveness was complete, a casual encounter with the perpetrators would bring a painful twinge inside me as a reminder that there was more work to be done. By the time I left the church for my next appointment, I had forgiven all those who had wronged me. I am certain that such forgiveness came more from God than from pure self will. Without God and the prodding of the gospel's command to forgive, I might still be angry with those who brought me such pain.

During the next few months I tried diligently to avoid using the pulpit as an avenue to express my anger. Even so, I knew I needed to address some of the issues that had surfaced through that tumultuous event: the specific role of the pastor, the church's identity, the responsibility of the laity for the health of the church, and the need for reconciliation and forgiveness. By the time I left that congregation I felt that I had worked through my pain and anger. Equally important, I believe the congregation was no longer in conflict with each other over the event. They were now ready to receive a new pastor—and to receive that minister with a clearer understanding of the pastor's role in the church.

Earlier in my ministry I had been on the other side of forgiveness—not the side of giving forgiveness but that of receiving it. A church member had accused me falsely concerning my motives when I arrived at the nursing home

Spiritual Mandates for Survival

after the death of his aunt. I had come to give support and to offer a prayer. But for some reason he thought I had come by in order to improve my chances of officiating at the funeral. During the next few months I tried in vain to convince him that my motives had been pure. After a while I simply gave him his space, believing I would never be able to change his mind. He and his wife continued to come to church but I sensed from his aloofness that he still blamed me for a wrong I had not committed.

A week before I was to leave the church I got a call from this estranged member. "My wife and I would like to have you and your family over for lunch after the service this Sunday!" To be honest, this was not my first choice for a farewell meal. I joked with my wife that if we were served mushroom soup, we should eat it very slowly and in fear of our lives!

The gathering for the meal was cordial and relaxed. No words of apology were ever spoken. Even so, I knew the real purpose for our time together. It meant that regardless of the member's assessment of me, he was not going to let me leave without reconciliation. As my wife and I drove away, I was comforted in knowing that one who had once thought ill of me had given me his final blessing.

It occurs to me that Holy Communion offers that same possibility—the gift of forgiveness and the bestowing of a blessing. Those who gather may come as friends or as enemies. But as we leave, we go in grace and with the blessing of Christ. But what is intended by this sacrament is even more—that we will go also with the blessing of each other. If so, the words first spoken as the bread is placed in our hands, "the Body of Christ," can then be spoken of us as a reconciled and forgiving community—"the body of Christ." Indeed.

QUESTIONS FOR REFLECTION

- Has forgiveness ever been a problem for you? Are there church members whom you have failed to forgive?

- Do you expect contrition before granting forgiveness? What if contrition never comes?

- What role has prayer played in your acts of forgiveness? Have you ever prayed for your enemies? If so, what effect, if any, did it have?

Spiritual Mandates for Survival

LET GO OF RESENTMENT FROM PAST IRRITATIONS!

It may feel good to lick our wounds, but it feels even better when they heal.

In talking with couples going through divorce, I have concluded that they are often doing so for one of two reasons: they are splitting up because of an act of betrayal or serious wrongdoing (big issues), or they are separating because over the years they have suffered countless irritations (small issues) until the irritations have evolved into resentment and thus eroded their affection. In ministry I have concluded that it is sometimes easier to let go of hurt when I can name both the offense and the offender, than to let go of resentment which has accumulated over the years from less serious infractions and from a variety of persons. In the first instance, I have only to forgive the person who has wronged me to find release. In the second case, the resentment has been tucked away over years of ministry and is not easily dissolved. With such resentment there is a pervasive pain, but the exact source of that pain is not clear and by then many of the co-conspirators have neither names nor faces. One is left with only an oppressive and persistent dis-ease. I can and do forgive persons who have wronged me. But how can I rid myself of a nebulous discomfort that has begun to stifle my playful spirit? How can I let go of resentment that once began as only a few blisters but now, through neglect, is a full-blown infection?

One year I found myself in a counselor's office trying to deal with the hurt of a carefully orchestrated "ambush" from a few misguided church members. I had gone to the counselor for help in dealing with my anger over one of the most traumatic events in my ministry. During second or third session, the counselor turned to me and asked: "Do you realize you have spent most of your time not talking about your recent attack but about your resentment stemming from a previous appointment?" Before dealing with the recent trauma, I would have to diffuse the left-over resentment from much less serious offenses. Eventually I would be set free from both types of resentments—those stemming from specific events and those caused from the accumulation of irritations and frustrations over the years.

One of the built-in dangers of being a minister is that we are apt to deny or ignore feelings of anger and irritation because we are afraid we might over-react, jeopardizing our ministry. So out of caution we suppress our anger or irritation. We may "turn the other cheek" showing no outward reaction but forget to let go of our resentment in the process. If we bury our resentment rather than owning it and then letting it go, over time we may produce a powder keg ready to blow. More likely, however, it will not explode but instead just smolder beneath the surface, hidden from view but not without wielding its destructive damage upon us and our ministry.

I wish I could give a precise step-by-step process for ridding oneself of long-term resentment. The best I can do is to suggest a straight-forward imperative expressed in a variety of ways: "Let it go! Stop reliving it! Stop rehearsing it, and stop whining about the unfairness of it all! Get over it! Or as an old-time mobster might put it: 'Fogettaboudit!'"

I remember one week deciding to preach on patience. Ever since then I have been cautious about choosing sermon topics. I am a bit skittish because after deciding to preach on patience, I have never before or since had my patience put to the test more. One day that week I was leaving the hospital parking lot when the guard at the gate asked for proof that I was a minister. I had no business card with me so I pointed to the clergy sticker on my rear window which had once been used for clergy parking there. She did not lift the gate. *Did she think I*

Spiritual Mandates for Survival

borrowed the car from my minister to avoid paying for parking? Becoming irritated, I asked for her name. She refused to tell me. *Did she think I could not find that out after I left?* By this time, however, she must have known I might report her so she let me go—but not happily or politely. As I drove off I realized that I had not exhibited the kind of "patience" I would be preaching about that Sunday. I also knew I was very upset, more upset than I should have been from the incident. As I turned the corner onto the main street, a quote I had heard recently came to mind: "Why should someone else's bad behavior ruin my day?" The sheer logic of that question sunk in. I took a deep breath and tried to leave my anger where I had first found it—on the parking lot. Perhaps the lady at the parking booth was attempting the same ritual.

Just "letting it go" remains my best advice for dealing with resentment, but there is something else one can do to mitigate the extent of collateral damage: always limit resentment's shelf life. The longer the resentment is retained, the harder it is to diffuse. So to prevent months and years in the resentment landfill, watch for the early signs of its accumulation: moodiness, exhaustion, unprovoked anger, a vulnerable self esteem. When resentment is finally diagnosed, try to name the cause or causes, and then let the resentment go. If you cannot resolve the resentment on your own, seek out a counselor, spouse, or friend to help you do so. Both your mental and spiritual lives depend on it.

I'm still not sure how I finally let go of my recurring resentment for the multitude of minor irritations that had permeated my life in ministry. I just know I did let it go—not all at once, but not as long as it had taken to build up inside me. I'm sure, however, that it was not just by my willing it to happen. It must have happened in part by the grace of God.

Unresolved resentment in a minister's life can be as dangerous to one's calling as unresolved resentment is to a marriage. It can suck the life right out of you. It can endanger the inner child, making it difficult to laugh and play and to be one's true self. It can even create mild depression. I am grateful that in those middle years of ministry, I finally learned not to bury irritations no matter how minor they seemed at the time. I learned not to build up resentment or to hold on to past hurt. I know all too well the damage such retention can cause. It can ruin a marriage, endanger a ministry, and stunt our spiritual growth. In short, it is not worth holding on to resentment just for the pleasure of tenderly nursing our injured feelings. Besides, why should the bad behavior of others ruin our lives? Indeed!

QUESTIONS FOR REFLECTION

- Do you agree with the author that letting go of resentment over a multitude of minor offenses is sometimes as hard as granting forgiveness for a serious wrong?

- What is your average "shelf life" for irritations? Do irritations ever evolve into long-term resentment?

- What methods do you use to keep irritations and frustrations from accumulating? Has resentment ever led to mild depression?

- How well do you handle the ordinary frustrations and irritations of life? Do you let them go easily or do you take out your frustration on the people around you?

Thriving in Ministry

CHAPTER THREE

FINDING FIRM FOUNDATIONS

GOD EMPOWERS MINISTRY!

Counting on our own strength leaves us short-handed and long-faced!

From the beginning of my ministry I believed that God empowered my ministry—and most especially in sermon preparation. Week after week in the crafting of sermons, I experienced God's guidance and inspiration. I instinctively knew that the sermonic ideas that came to my consciousness were not merely my creations alone. But as I began to feel more intensely the weight of ministerial office and life, I sometimes carried the various ministerial responsibilities as if they rested solely and squarely upon my shoulders. I knew I had a partner in ministry but I acted more as one *sent* rather than *empowered*. When overwhelmed with the tasks ahead, I sometimes approached the challenge with either heroic effort (I will do it!) or with reduced expectation (I don't see how I can do it but I will try). Few over-conscientious ministers will ever admit to such cloaked idolatry, but all too many of us go about our job as if its success were ours alone to seize. Our stressed-out profession is a towering witness to our misguided egotistical mindset.

Most ministers will certainly encounter from time to time a ministerial role or work load that is obviously too heavy to manage alone. I had many such instances scattered throughout my ministry but few as dramatic as the one that came in my third appointment. At first glance, the general responsibilities at that church were not overwhelming. The church was small enough to be manageable and large enough to have adequate lay involvement. And by then I had honed a few skills, become a bit wiser, and had several models for ministry carefully stored inside my clergy toolbox. The challenge I would face there would not be in programming, administration, or general pastoral care—all of these had very reasonable demands. My taxing load would come in the area of worship, which was probably my stronger skill set at the time.

The problem was not in planning any particular service whether it was Sunday morning or evening worship or a funeral service. The issue was in the sheer number of these services and their accompanying sermons—all requiring significant planning, crafting, and execution. Unlike urban churches, this county-seat church still had a formal Sunday night service in addition to Sunday morning worship. I also conducted a different style worship service for a satellite church that met eleven miles away. Even this significant weekly work load was manageable until one added the frequent funerals, which averaged thirty to forty a year.

I will never forget the challenge of one particular week in my second year there. During that momentous week I would be required to prepare six worship services and five sermons, all in addition to my other ministerial duties and family responsibilities. Only one of these sermons had any advance work prior to that week—the one for Sunday morning. The funeral sermons would draw heavily from the times I spent with the families at the time of the deaths and during family conferences. As I faced the formidable responsibility for the week, I knew I would somehow "live through it" but I was concerned that I would not be able to prepare adequately for all of the services. It seemed an almost impossible task.

After completing the two funerals on Tuesday and one on Thursday, I began to feel a bit more hopeful, especially since all three services seem to have been meaningful to the families and to those gathered in love and support. For the next two days I put most of my work into finishing the plans for the Sunday morning service and its sermon. After the two services on Sunday morning, one at the main church and one at the satellite church, I was emotionally and physically spent. After the Sunday noon meal I still had one more sermon and service to plan with only hours to complete them. Unfortunately I had little more than a text and a gem of a sermon idea as I began my sacred task.

After the evening service was over I locked up the church and headed for the parsonage. Surprisingly, even the evening service had gone well. It was certainly not my best sermon, but it had substance and passion and was reasonably well received. Few at the service would have any idea about the short incubation time of that sermon. Two hours of preparation are rarely adequate for any sermon, but as I headed for the house the mantra of my father seemed somehow appropriate—"good enough."

That week's experience became a powerful "aha moment" for me. It reminded me of what I already knew but too often ignored—God would always empower me to do the work he called me to do. I did not have to carry all of the responsibility because I had a partner in ministry—not an associate, but an awesome ever-present God.

I suppose a common pitfall in ministry is to fail to trust in God's empowerment of our ministry. We sometimes foolishly act as if we are in control. We sometime labor as though the effectiveness of our ministry is primarily up to us.

We substitute heroic conscientiousness for faithfulness. But ministry has a way of reminding us that the task is too large to balance on our shoulders alone. More often than we would like, a week in the life of the church is clearly beyond our pay grade. We are forced to look beyond our own resources. Hopefully, we will ask for help and receive it; hopefully, we will not have to have another crisis before we seek God's empowerment again.

Of course there is another danger in how we share our ministerial load. Instead of thinking we must do most of the work, the other danger is that we will expect God to do most of the work. Such abandonment of responsibility is like a person who refuses to study for a test and then prays for a high grade; or even worse, a minister who does little sermon preparation and then asks God to provide the words for the message. God empowers our ministry—to be sure—but he still expects us to put out the effort and do our part.

Before leaving this subject of God's empowerment, I feel compelled to also point out that God's empowerment is directed specifically toward our work in ministry, toward God's purposes. The promise of empowerment is not intended as a means of securing our own agenda and goals. Nor is God's empowerment intended for our professional advancement or financial gain. It takes only a quick survey of biblical characters to conclude that service to God is not often accompanied with great material or personal gain. Most of God's servants, in fact, followed God's will at great personal sacrifice.

Some of the stress of ministry comes from our tendency to treat our various tasks as if most of the responsibility for their success is ours. Too often we foolishly forget that God offers his people and his leaders more than his presence; he offers his power as well. When I am facing a heavy work load, I sometimes think back to that week so long ago—six services and five sermons. Wow! If God can empower me to produce

Finding Firm Foundations

meaningful and effective work in such demanding circumstances, surely he can help me with other challenges that threaten to overwhelm me! I am now wary of putting my trust only in my honed skills and heroic efforts. Such tactics will leave me nothing less than shorthanded and long-faced!

Thriving in Ministry

QUESTIONS FOR REFLECTION

- After a most difficult week as pastor have you ever believed that without God's empowerment you could not have succeeded?

- How do you strike the balance in your work between putting too must trust in yourself and expecting too much from God?

- Do you ever find yourself claiming to believe in God's empowerment of ministry but acting as if the responsibility is mostly yours?

DEVELOP STRONG FRIENDSHIPS WITHIN THE CLERGY FAMILY!

No one else will fully understand the trials, stresses, and joys of ministry.

Being a transfer from the Little Rock Annual Conference, the only ministers I knew that first year of ministry were the few who interviewed me from the Board of Ordained Ministry. One of those ministers, some twenty years my senior, called and invited my wife and me for coffee after the evening worship at the annual conference in Dallas. We were thrilled to accept. I finally knew someone in the conference! Unfortunately, my new friend in ministry was assigned to a church hours away and in a year or so would be transferred out of the conference.

During my first two years of appointment, I was able to meet a few ministers at district meetings. Most were much older and none became my close friends. My next appointment would be a church of my own located in a town of fourteen hundred people. The few ministers I knew were now miles away. My wife and I did manage to meet two families in the town and we became friends, enjoying games of forty-two and just hanging out. Later they would surprise me by walking down the aisle together to join the church.

During our second year in the small town a clergy couple about ten years older invited us to their parsonage for dinner. We soon discovered they had a very specific agenda for the visit. No, thank goodness, they were not trying to sell us something. After the meal they got right to the point by giving us their passionate advice: "Find friends in ministry—close friends." We made a few excuses about not yet finding close friends in ministry and said we planned to just find friends in the churches we served or in the community. They were not at all impressed with our friendship plan and repeated their mantra a second time: "Find friends in ministry. They will be the only ones who can really understand what it is like to be in ministry. We can be those friends, or someone else can be your friends, but trust us—you will need friends in the clergy!"

Within two years we moved to a county seat town and had not yet taken the couple's advice. We still had no close clergy friends but at least by now we knew many of the minister families in the district and some we had been able to visit with at the district gatherings. But our new appointment setting offered little opportunity for friendships, with very few people our age with kids. (We now had two.)

One day my wife shocked me with a somewhat desperate statement. Ordinarily, she had a very positive attitude and upbeat personality. At that time in our marriage (about seven years) I could not remember her ever being emotionally down for more than a day or two—at least, I had not been *aware* of such despondency. On that eventful day she looked into my eyes and spoke calmly but emphatically: "Justin, I'm depressed. We have no friends. I'm dying here. We have to do something!"

Before the day was over we had a plan. We invited two couples to come to our house for dinner. Both families served in churches in the area about 30 minutes away. Our strategy was to have the dinner, share our problem of isolation, and ask if they would be willing to get together once a month for an indefinite period of time. If they did not share the same need, perhaps they could just do us a favor.

The gathering itself was a creative one—a hobo party. Everyone was to come wearing their shabbiest clothes. My wife covered the den furniture and floor with newspaper. The meal was served out of tin cans using plastic spoons with everyone sitting on the floor. It was a fun time for all, even for the kids. At supper we made our impassioned plea for their help and

Finding Firm Foundations

both couples readily agreed. One couple volunteered for the next get-together and we all grabbed our calendars and set the date.

At our second time together we ate the evening meal at the kitchen table and then talked while the kids entertained themselves. After putting them down for the night we continued visiting until two o'clock in the morning when someone finally suggested we had better get some sleep. We were up again early the next morning, had a quick breakfast and resumed our conversation at the kitchen table until the kids started complaining they were hungry for lunch. It was then we noticed that we were still in our pajamas and robes! It was now official: "The Tulls were not the only ones in need of fellowship!" Perhaps we all knew as we went our separate ways that this was the beginning of a friendship, but none of us could have envisioned how deep a friendship it would become.

It has now been some thirty-six years since that first hobo party. The group (or "the Gang" as we came to call ourselves) has not met every month but we have probably averaged six times a year for over three decades. Our group has added other couples to our fellowship from time to time but the first three couples stayed constant. We have shared meals together with an assortment of culinary delights: hot dogs, fried alligator, pork chops with sauce of gold, black-eyed pea soup, bread pudding, Cajun fish, lemon angel pie—just to name a few. We have taken trips together with all or part of the group present: Paris, Texas and Paris, France; Cooper and Wolfe City, Texas; Fayetteville and Little Rock, Arkansas. We have done marriage enrichment trips, canoe trips, fishing trips, and stayed together in a cabin in Colorado. We have celebrated almost every holiday except Ground Hog Day, and that may someday happen.

Best of all, we have shared most of the watershed moments of our lives, including the marriage of our children, the funerals of our parents, the birth and baptism of our grandchildren. Often one of us would serve as the officiating minister on these occasions. We have also offered each other support through countless illnesses, surgeries, and close encounters with death. In my case, these friends were with my wife, Lynn, and me as she battled a terminal illness. These faithful ones visited and supported us until the very end. They continued to support me in my days as a widower, calling me often and checking on me. They even hosted a birthday party for me. Years later, when I remarried, they offered the best wedding present they could have given us—a place for my wife, Janette, in the long-established circle of friends. Janette would not be Lynn's replacement, but a person in her own right. She would hear the best of all the old stories, the best and the worst of the jokes, and would begin building her own memories as the group travelled together to California, Greece and Turkey.

I suppose what I treasure most about these friends in the ministry is that they are the "historians of my life." They know more about me than my parents have known. They have been present at almost every crisis and every crowning moment of my adult life. They know me more than anyone else except the two women who agreed to marry me. These wonderful people, with whom I have shared my life, know who I really am, and still love me.

I would not suggest that having clergy friends will often evolve into such close relationships. Some people may even find the thought of such closeness a bit stifling. But if one can find close friends who just happen to be in ministry, then it is likely to evolve into something special. Who else can tell those hilarious accounts of the mishaps at weddings, funerals, baptisms, and Holy Communion? To some, these stories may

Finding Firm Foundations

seem sacrilegious, but to people of the cloth they are just the comic side of a life that has surrounded us and sometimes overwhelmed us.

Each year I witness the coming in of new ministers into our conference. I am tempted to invite each one over for dinner and repeat a speech I heard some forty years ago: "Find close friends in ministry. No one will understand your life better than those who have been called into this sacred adventure." I could invite them all over and share my advice—or perhaps, I could just write a book and tell them.

QUESTIONS FOR REFLECTION

- Have you found close clergy friends? If not, are you inclined to do so?

- Do you have friends in your church? Do you share with them your true self?

- Do you have friends from former churches you have served? What rules, if any, do you follow in maintaining these friendships without intruding into the role of the present pastor?

- What do you look for in a close friend?

Allow the Saints to Cheer You On!

Many will pray for us, minister to us, and love us—if we let them!

Two of my favorite symbols of ministry are captured in two *Precious Moments* figurines. One is of a preacher with a sunny-side-up egg on top of his head standing behind a rough wooden pulpit covered with splattered tomatoes. Around the base of the figurine is written a passage of scripture familiar to all in the profession: "If God be for us, who can be against us (Romans 8:31b)?" It is a perfect representation of the vulnerability of the ministerial office.

The second figurine is a soldier outfitted with medieval head gear and shield and brandishing a sword. You guessed it: "Onward Christian Soldiers" is its title. The angelic face of the soldier, complete with band-aid, suggests that a battle had been waged amidst danger and at the cost of injury. The figurine has great meaning to me since it was given by an elderly clergy spouse, one familiar with the vulnerabilities of ministry. She was also quite aware that I was fending off a few aggressive church members. It was reassuring that she understood my plight and offered both her empathy and support. It also helped that the figurine had a somewhat comic tone, reminding me that I should not take my wounds too seriously. The porcelain figure, that would grace my study bookshelf for years, brought to my mind both humility and courage—traits that always wear well in ministry.

In earlier chapters I have bared my soul about the pain that often comes with ministry. In this short piece I want to share what has helped me stay in ministry and to be able to do so with a joyous and committed heart. I'm talking about the power of encouragement that has been showered upon me at times of my greatest need.

As I think about those who have cheered me on, several people stand out in my mind—people whose timing and generosity were life-saving, like the widow who gave me the Christian soldier figurine. One lady, however, stands unmatched by her extravagant gestures. At a time of some of my deepest pain in ministry, I received a cut crystal bowl crammed with three dozen tulips. A small arrangement would not do. Later during somewhat better days, our family received her Christmas present: a huge box of chocolates. These were no ordinary chocolates—they were hand-made by a specialty shop. And the quality of the chocolates was certainly matched by the quantity—ten pounds! Do you know how hard it is to eat ten pounds of chocolates? For the next month, any visitor who did not belong to the church received a generous portion of our gift until our ample stash was depleted. Surprisingly, long after the chocolates were gone, its sweet taste lingered with its savory message: "You are loved and appreciated." The gift was given by one person but it felt like a gift of love from the whole church.

Some churches have learned well how to offer love and support to their pastor family. The photo on the front cover displays the sanctuary of such a church. When I was serving there I was amazed at the number of living saints on our rolls. The church was already known as the highest per capita giving church in the conference. What many did not realize is that it also had, in my opinion, the highest per capita of saints in the conference. Their faith and their faithfulness were a constant inspiration to me. Their words of encouragement helped me grow as a person and as a pastor.

But sometimes such love and support are not known to us. I was asked to do the memorial service for one of our saints, an elderly woman whose quiet and gentle nature was apparent to all in the church. Interns at the church would often sit beside

Finding Firm Foundations

her as she volunteered to answer the phone. In planning for her service I visited with the family and marveled at the stories of her loving and non-judgmental influence on children and grandchildren alike. Before I left that evening a member of the family brought me a worn scrap of paper. It was wrinkled and faded from perhaps years of use. "It's her prayer list," they told me. I glanced down at the piece of paper not yet making out the names listed, perhaps fifteen or twenty of them written in pencil. "Look at the top of the list," they suggested. I looked and was stunned by what I saw. At the top of the piece of paper was my name. "It was her daily prayer sheet," they told me, reminding me that prayer was never an afterthought for her. The image of her praying on my behalf swept over me. I was deeply touched that she had prayed for me every day of my ministry from the time I arrived until the day she died. I was both humbled and honored.

As a pastor in the trenches I may choose to dwell on the hurts of ministry. But if I do so, I had better take full note of all the saints who have always been on my side! In the Christian faith we have a word for that kind of encouragement which may be offered from both sides of eternity. We call it the "cloud of witnesses" and it offers us its passionate encouragement as we run the race set before us.

I am comforted by the thought of all those daily prayers during my ministry at her church. I also draw comfort in believing that death did not put an end to her sacred practice. Somewhere in the immediate and intimate presence of God, I envision this dear saint kneeling with her new prayer card, still offering up her love and concern for people in another realm. I would not presume that my name still tops her list, but I am bold enough to hope that I made the cut. I have no doubt that she and the great saints of the faith are cheering for all of us, and especially for those who have answered God's call. Thanks be to God.

QUESTIONS FOR REFLECTION

- Have extravagant gestures of encouragement ever lifted your spirits?

- What seems to affect your resolve the most, the barrage of negativity or the cheers of the saints?

- If those who encourage us lift our spirits, what effect must we have as we minister to the flock? What gestures have we offered that may have brought hope or encouragement to others?

- What is your understanding of the "community of the saints"?

CHAPTER FOUR

LEADERSHIP MANDATES

DON'T MAKE UNILATERAL DECISIONS!
We must request input from people affected by our decisions.

It did not take me long to make a major mistake in ministry. In my second year as associate minister with responsibilities for the youth program, I was faced with a decision about the graduating sixth grade class. As summer approached I was very concerned about how I could get this class involved in the youth program which included seventh through twelfth graders. It soon occurred to me that the obvious strategy would be to get them involved in the summer youth program so that when they started school the next year they would be committed to the youth group and already integrated into the fellowship. However, the long-time tradition of the church was that the sixth graders did not become a part of the youth program until September. In September the Sunday school classes were promoted to the new grades, and only then would the new seventh graders become a part of the evening youth program.

I was careful to discuss the issue of promoting the sixth graders early with all the adult counselors of the Sunday night youth program. We all agreed that it would be best to promote them into the youth group the first of June. But there was a problem. If we promoted them to the youth group, it would be

Leadership Mandates

awkward for these same classmates to stay in the sixth grade morning Sunday school class. After talking with the evening youth sponsors, I decided that it would be best to promote the sixth graders into seventh grade for both morning and evening programs. Being careful to follow proper procedure, I took my plan to the education committee and easily received their approval. They agreed we could break with tradition and move up the sixth graders to the seventh grade Sunday school class in June rather than September. The youth council also approved the early move for the Sunday night program.

When I finished getting the master plan approved, I was proud of myself for having gone through due process and for involving the various players and committees with the decision. My next step was to send out a letter to all the six graders and their parents. It still had not occurred to me that I had left out of the process one important party entirely—the teacher of the sixth grade Sunday school class. I had never even spoken to him about the plan. In fact, I think he had to hear about the planned move second hand. But though he did not hear directly from me, I can assure you that I soon heard in person from him. I got a call just after the letter went out. "Justin, I have a serious problem with your plan for moving up the sixth grade Sunday school class to the seventh grade class in June instead of September." (His voice was in control but conveyed a high level of both irritation and authority.) "Did it ever occur to you that I might have planned exactly what I wanted to teach these kids and that I might not be ready to let them go?" Of course, it had not occurred to me. I had not thought about how my plan would affect his teaching at all.

The teacher was upset and the worse part about it was I knew his irritation was totally justified. I had made a change to a program that affected him greatly without even so much as a phone call. I immediately apologized to him and said I had made a mistake. I asked what he wanted me to do about it. "I want it back the way it was," he said. I agreed.

In a few weeks I would revisit the education committee. We voted to promote the sixth graders into the junior high youth group in June but kept them in the sixth grade Sunday school class until promotion Sunday at the first of September. After resending the vote, it took me a while to smooth out my relationship with the sixth grade Sunday school teacher, but he did forgive me and in my remaining time there became a strong supporter of the youth program. I'm sure it helped that I admitted I had been wrong and that I reversed the decision. But I give him credit for graciously handing a young minister a "get out of jail free" card.

What did I learn that second year of ministry? One is not a good leader if one makes decisions without involving the people who will be affected. In other words: *Don't make unilateral decisions.* It is not enough to have pure motives and good intentions. It is not enough to involve *some* people in the process; we must be careful to include all the people affected by a decision. If one ever makes a similar mistake, I have some advice. *Take the heat; offer an apology; make it right.* I did not easily forget the embarrassment of having to undo a month's worth of work because of my oversight. More importantly, I did not soon forget the undeserved hurt I had brought to someone who was a dedicated worker in the church. I pledged to do better in the years ahead, and I did.

Leadership Mandates

Questions for Reflection

- Does a pastor or church leader have the right to make unilateral decisions bypassing input from those affected by the decision?

- Have you ever made a unilateral decision that had negative consequences? Please explain.

- How does one allow feedback and input toward a decision without implying that the decision will be a simple matter of majority rule?

Dare to be a Manager!
*Be a mentor, supervisor, or the one who intervenes—
all depending on the staff member!*

My fifth church appointment was to a large church with a staff of nineteen people, several being part-time employees. The first staff meeting I ever attended was the one I would conduct in my new church. As youth director, I had participated in what we called "staff meetings" but their main purpose was simply to go over the church calendar. There was no effort at group building, no spiritual dimension except for an opening prayer, and no exchange of ideas to improve our work as a staff or church. Now, as senior pastor, I was the staff leader and it was my responsibility as to whether or not staff meetings had any substance. From the start, I wanted to be a "hands on" leader totally involved in the life of the church and supportive of the staff. I soon learned that I should not attempt to relate to each staff member in the same way. Each would require a different level of involvement based on their gifts, experience, personality, and mindset. Some would need mentoring and others would require supervision. Still others would simply need permission to do their jobs.

As a senior pastor I have especially enjoyed the role of mentor. When I came to the large church, I had already been a supervising pastor for an intern from Perkins School of Theology. Later in ministry I would supervise eight more interns. But it was late in my ministry when I enjoyed my most rewarding mentoring experience, this time not in a formal program, but by choice. I decided early in this particular appointment to invite the associate into my pastoral world as a true partner. Early on I shared all my goals and strategies with her while withholding such privileged information from the rest of the staff. I also depended heavily upon her insights into the

Leadership Mandates

congregation and for her feedback as to how the church was progressing. Because of the close professional relationship we enjoyed, she was able to get a glimpse into the unique role of senior pastor. A few years later these insights would be extremely helpful as she assumed the senior pastor role herself.

Our work together was not only one of mentoring but also a true partnership in ministry. Sometimes we shared parallel roles like preaching. Other times there was a clear division of responsibilities: she did programming where as I did none; she coordinated the liturgy and I just gave input; I took the majority of the pastoral care load and she supplemented that role. I handled all the key communications to the church and she gave feedback to all my rough drafts. In a true mentoring relationship, though one may have the advantage of experience (usually referred to as the mentor), the other brings a fresh look to the role so that both learn from the other. If a staff member has all the gifts and graces for a position but little experience, a mentoring model is often effective and sometimes necessary. It can be done formally with weekly meetings or informally through conversations and example.

Some staff members are not candidates for mentoring. They may require instead explicit direction from the senior pastor. Supervision is often used to monitor an employee that lacks experience or one who has demonstrated a certain weakness in performance. Supervision is more direct than mentoring and often uses the authority of the supervisory position to encourage improvement or leverage compliance. Even so, the supervisor is not to use a heavy hand unless the weakness or short-coming is a serious one.

In one large church appointment, I was given the opportunity to engage my supervisory function. My son was a part of the church youth group. I certainly did not send him to the group as a spy but I was glad he told me about a particular event that happened at the Sunday night youth activity. When he came home I could tell that he was upset but it took a while before he would tell me what happened. The youth director had shown the movie "Psycho" to the entire youth group including the seventh graders. My son was shaken by the scary movie. My first thought was to question showing a secular movie for the evening program. But my greatest concern was the youth director's inappropriate choice of movies, especially for the younger members of the group. When I talked to the youth director the next day he did not understand why I had a problem with the showing of the film. His defense was that he gave the younger ones a chance to opt out of seeing it. I countered by saying that no seventh grade boy would admit that he was afraid to watch a scary movie. I told him that since his judgment of an "appropriate film" differed so much from mine that I would have to approve any future films. I made a mental note that this staff member would have to be supervised perhaps in other areas as well. I sent a follow-up memo to him about the rule for movie selection. I also told him I did not like surprises—things blowing up with no warning ahead of time—so I would appreciate his coming to me ahead of time if he thought I might disapprove of some future program or activity. From that point on, I had no major problem with this staff member and the youth program continued as a stable endeavor.

In a more recent staff experience I had to use a more aggressive managerial technique: intervention. When I arrived at my new appointment, I soon discovered that one member of the staff had a history of being uncooperative with the rest of the staff and was sometimes even subversive in his behavior. He was definitely not a team player. When anything infringed at all on his space, his schedule, or his program he would act as though his ministry was the only one that mattered. The rest of the staff would just have to adjust to his program's needs.

Leadership Mandates

When it came time in the remodeling process to move all of the staff offices, he told the secretary who was orchestrating the process that it was not a good time for him to move his office. He said this even knowing that his failure to move would cause the business manager to be without phone and computer service until the move took place. Several days later he had still not moved. I decided intervention was in order. The lay leader and I met with him and the lay leader took the lead. "We will need to move your office this Wednesday. Do you want to do it or shall we do it for you?" He calmly opted to let us move him. I personally supervised the move, expecting that he might complain about how the job was done. My suspicions would soon be confirmed. Several days later I received word that he had sent out a memo to the youth and their parents complaining that when he arrived at his office on Wednesday night he was shocked to discover that his stuff had been moved and that his computer did not work—and he was upset! (In other words, he implied in his letter that his office had been moved without his knowledge and that it had not been done properly.) The letter suggested that he was the victim of the staff's actions. I even got a complaint after the letter went out that we should not have been so unfair to this wonderful staff person! I then shared my side of the story.

I met the next day with the staff member telling him that he would be appearing before the Staff Parish Relations Committee to explore his lack of cooperation with the workings of the staff. A copy of his letter would be read. I told him his days of sabotage were over and that I would see that he cooperated when other groups and other staff members needed to use space that he sometimes used. He would no longer be allowed to hold the staff hostage to his wishes. He later met with Staff Parish and unsuccessfully defended his actions. Not surprisingly, within about six months this staff member found another job. Prima Donnas do not work well when they can no longer get their way.

Staff intervention, when it is necessary, is the responsibility of the senior pastor or the executive pastor. This does not mean that the pastor must be the one who confronts or makes demands. I always want the backing of the Staff Parish Relations Committee so that whatever action is taken will be seen as a church decision and not the result of a personal conflict between a staff member and me. In intervention the issue often cannot be resolved by mentoring or supervising because the root cause may be a character flaw, in this case the staff member being totally self-absorbed if not narcissistic. I have found that the best way to "manage" such staff members is to simply hold them accountable for their behavior, make that behavior known to the personnel committee, and develop a complete paper trail of the problematic issues in case termination is later required. I sometimes refer to this method as "tightening the screws." This method requires more and more improvement or compliance from the staff member until often he or she decides to find another job elsewhere. Often this method has less collateral damage than if this person is simply terminated. In the later case the terminated staff member will often play the "victim" card, causing many church members to take sides. The disadvantage to the "tightening of the screws" method is that it often takes time. If the poor staff performance is causing too much damage in the meantime, then that method must be replaced with immediate termination.

QUESTIONS FOR REFLECTION

- If you have a staff at present, make a list of who is a candidate for mentoring, who needs to be supervised, who needs to be held accountable or admonished, and who needs to be supported and set free to do the job. How will you show respect to the staff in the way you execute each of these styles?

- Have you ever had a mentor? What were the most helpful insights you gained from your mentoring experience? What methods did the mentor use?

- Have you ever had to confront a staff member who was causing problems with the staff? What methods did you use and were they successful?

- What is the difference between a character flaw and a weakness? Should they be treated differently?

Resist the Temptation to Over-Manage!
Micromanaging wastes time, hampers productivity, and creates low morale!

In the last chapter I suggested that proper church management requires significant involvement of the senior pastor. Mentoring, supervising, and intervening are all necessary leadership styles to improve the life of the staff and ultimately the health of the church. To fail to take such responsibility is a terrible neglect of the ministerial office. However, to over-function in that role can be equally detrimental to the workings of the staff and to the role of senior pastor.

Instead of leading the staff, some senior pastors try to take over the staff—insisting on having the final say as much as possible. There are many reasons why micromanaging is a bad practice. Listed below are a few reasons micromanaging is unadvisable:

- If a senior pastor is doing everything in his or her job description to the fullest, little time remains for trying to second guess everyone else's work.
- Meddling in everybody's business is mostly a waste of time because it discounts the value of staff members and inevitably leads to frustration and low staff morale. If the pastor is always tweaking the work of the entire staff, this will be seen as a lack of confidence in their ability.
- If the senior pastor is intruding in everyone's work, the staff will become more cautious and less creative in order to avoid needless correction.
- If several staff members need intense supervision and constant monitoring from the senior pastor, then sometimes it is more practical to terminate the incompetent employees and start over.

Leadership Mandates

- Persons with "character flaws" (dishonesty, narcissistic behavior, deep-seated authority problems, prima donna complex) can rarely be transformed into good staff members through strict supervision or extreme micromanaging.

So if one agrees that micromanaging is almost always a bad thing, how can we recognize it when we do it? A simple questionnaire can help. (Answer "yes" or "no" as to which is the most accurate description of your normal behavior.)

1. Do you sometimes try to gain control of jobs assigned to a staff member?
2. Do you criticize part of a staff member's plan without expressing anything positive about it?
3. Do you fail to show respect for the work of the other person by always insisting on "tweaking" it?
4. Rather than making "suggestions" of changes to a staff member's plan, do you simply "instruct" them to make the changes you suggested?
5. Do you offer very minor suggestions to a staff member's plan when it will make little difference to the project?
6. Do you make regular suggestions to staff members on how they are to do their jobs?
7. Do you often sense resistance or irritation from the staff when you make suggestions?

If you answered "yes" to three or more to these questions, then you are probably guilty of some micromanaging.

When I took an assignment as an interim minister there were a few times I was tempted to micromanage even though I did not have time for much beyond my major responsibilities.

When I came on the scene as the new senior interim minister, the associate and the music director had been planning the worship liturgy and selecting the hymns. At first I thought I should meet with them, get their feedback, give my input and eventually make some minor changes in worship. After all, I was now in charge of worship and I had gifts in that area. But as I visited with the two staff members about worship I sensed they wanted to continue their primary role in worship planning. They did not readily support the few suggestions I offered in our meetings. In a few weeks I made the decision to play only a minor role in the designing of worship. My role became primarily sharing in advance my sermon text, title and the theme of the service. I allowed them to do the final planning and mockup. The only exception to this was in planning for the special Christian seasons where we all gave input into the design and component parts. They remained, however, the ones who did all the finishing touches.

My decision not to micromanage worship was a very wise choice. It improved my relationship with these two staff members by showing my trust in them. (I rarely saw the completed liturgy before Sunday morning.) More importantly, it freed me from one area of work and allowed me more time for such things as preaching and pastoral care. Micromanaging can sometimes, in the short run, actually improve the "product." In the long run, however, it often does more harm than good. Good ministerial practice would be to micromanage rarely and only then as a last resort.

Leadership Mandates

Questions for Reflection

- Can you name a time when your supervision evolved into micromanaging? Was the shift justified?

- Have you ever micromanaged a person who should have been fired instead?

- When is "tweaking" someone else's work justified? What approach would one use?

- Do you allow staff members enough freedom to fail? Why or why not? Please share an example of either stepping in to fix a potential problem, or stepping back to allow risk of failure.

BUILD A TEAM!

*Establish a microcosm of the church—
a healthy one!*

For some time now I have seen the church staff as a microcosm of the church. As a staff leader, one of my jobs is to help the staff become a healthy team willing to work together and offer support to each other. The health of the church staff can certainly influence the general health of the church. In like manner, if the staff is riddled with power plays and uncaring behavior it can have a negative effect of the spiritual life of the church at large.

When I arrived at an interim appointment following the tragic death of a young and beloved pastor, I knew the staff could help the congregation work through grief if they were able to process their own grief. Similarly, if the staff showed signs of melancholy and depression, it would adversely affect the healing of the church. I encouraged the staff to show signs of hope, renewal, and a fresh spirit so that the congregation would be given permission to move forward and process their grief. As the staff leader, I offered my support to them, knowing that they had carried a very heavy load for some time. I met individually with each member of the staff. I suggested that they should get help if they needed it. Though the work load was still very intense, I also encouraged them to take some time off as they could. Physical exhaustion can delay the grief process.

As a whole the staff did a wonderful job of facing their sense of loss and thereby becoming able to minister to a hurting congregation. Their concern for the members of the church helped them heal. The church also did a remarkable job in handling such a tragic circumstance. Part of their success was due to the good example and loving support by the staff.

Leadership Mandates

In looking back over my church appointments, I observed a direct correlation between the health of the staff and the health of the church. My least effective appointment was at a church where I was never able to build a healthy team spirit.

In building a church staff, there are several actions and principles worthy of adoption:

- Decide what style of management is needed for each staff member: mentoring, supervising, intervening, or simply supporting.
- Treat everyone with respect and expect each staff member to treat co-workers the same way.
- Praise in public and criticize in private.
- Inform staff members that you do not like to be "blind-sided." Staff members should always alert the senior pastor in advance about new programs, activities, policies that might cause controversy or problems.
- Make clear that "It's not my job!" is not an acceptable response to requests. Lead by example by demonstrating that no job is beneath the role of senior pastor.
- Make sure there are comprehensive job descriptions for each staff position and use them in the evaluation process.
- Have staff members write their own performance evaluations and incorporate them into your evaluation of their work.
- Make training available to each staff member to improve job performance.
- Give regular feedback to staff members about their work. Never forget to affirm good work.
- Offer pastoral support to staff members, especially in times of difficulty.
- Be an advocate for proper benefits and financial compensation for staff members.

Thriving in Ministry

- Be creative with staff budgets and division of responsibilities, realigning staff assignments when necessary.
- Make staff meetings a time of spiritual growth, team building, and visioning—as well as a time to take care of current ministries and programming.
- If there are tensions between staff members, invite them to work it out themselves and intervene if necessary.
- Claim the role of leader while using group process to improve ideas.
- Strive to treat each staff person fairly, avoiding playing favorites.
- Use humor and celebration as a way to build the team and to suggest that there should be joy in the midst of church work.

Leadership Mandates

QUESTIONS FOR REFLECTION

- What role does the spiritual health of the staff play in the spiritual health and well-being of the church?

- Pick your favorite three principles for building a church staff and tell why you chose them.

- What keys would you list for good staff relations? List at least two of your own principles and offer support for your choices.

STAY CONNECTED TO ENEMIES AND LEADERSHIP!
We can keep our integrity without keeping our distance.

I had been a minister for some time before I realized it was often smart to stay connected to those who posed a threat to my ministry. Prior to that time, I tended to keep my distance from those who did not like me or from those who opposed my style of ministry. In one church that practice of "intentional distance" may have contributed to a lay person's opposition to my ministry. Upon arriving at the church, I was asked by a church member to join Rotary. He also requested that he accompany me to the meetings. By then I had concluded that he was a power broker in the church and I became leery of his motives. After about a year I dropped out of Rotary and consequently had little contact with him except at church meetings. Later, as chair of the nominations committee, I would fail to secure for him a place on the Board when he rotated out of a key leadership position. My failure to nominate him for some position, even a much reduced one, was a serious oversight. Had I continued my early relationship with him I doubt that I would have failed to include him on the Board. A year later he would be instrumental in my departure from the church. Had I paid just some attention to him, I think his attitude toward me would have been different. He might have even been an on-going supporter of my ministry.

The longer in ministry, the more committed I became to stay connected to those who were not my biggest fans. In fact, I believe it is a good idea for all pastors to stay connected to people who are not supportive of their ministry. If we isolate ourselves from them, it could be interpreted as a direct threat, making them even more dangerous to us and to the church. Keeping in touch with those who oppose us also keeps us keenly aware of their attitudes and actions. In some rare cases,

Leadership Mandates

staying connected may even lead to a positive relationship or at least one of mutual respect. Isolation almost guarantees an ongoing stand-off.

In one church I attended a meeting concerning the youth. A parent spoke out about the youth program and suggested that the type of worship practiced by the church could not reach the youth. As I listened to his numerous comments during the meeting, I formed a very clear impression of him. I decided that I did not like him, or this theology or his taste in worship styles. For some reason, however, I called him the next day and invited him to meet with me at my office. When he sat down to visit, I asked him to share his general impressions of the church and what he thought the problems were in our current crisis. (The church had recently lost a third of its attendance and giving prior to my coming.) As he spoke I suddenly became open to what he was saying rather than preparing my rebuttal. I also sensed from him an openness to me and a willingness to listen to my insights about the church. After a long time together he offered his blessing on my ministry. Later he would call me to say he had finally decided to transfer his membership to a church he had been visiting for some time. (I had learned earlier that he had been unhappy with this home church but had not been able to make a decision to leave.) He also told me his two teenagers were going to remain at the church until they graduated from high school. I felt good that our conversation had helped him make a decision about both his church needs and those of his children. Although he would be leaving the church, he would be doing so not in anger or frustration but by blessing both me and the future of the church. Of all the people I talked to during my appointment there, this person, whom I initially strongly disliked, gave me more helpful insights into the church and its identity than any other person including the key church leaders. I learned from this experience that sometimes those who seem to be our enemies can help us see weaknesses and dynamics that others cannot discern. As I look back on that church experience, I am so glad I was willing to talk to someone with whom I strongly disagreed. He truly helped me understand the dynamics of the church and thus enhanced my ministry there.

Staying connected to our enemies may seem like a radical idea. Staying connected with our leadership just sounds like common sense. Yet even with key leadership, I sometimes related to leadership more on a personal or pastoral level rather than as leader to leader. During my ministry I prided myself in not being too "political." I did not meet with members of committees behind the scenes prior to a meeting to help insure the passage of a proposal. My normal practice was to rely mainly on my input at the meeting itself. I sometimes failed to be persuasive in a meeting because I had not attempted to bring people on board ahead of time. I suppose I thought that would have been was too "political." Occasionally I would even fail to give the chair of a committee a detailed "heads-up" about what I would be presenting at the next meeting. Strangely enough, I hated being "blindsided." at staff meetings. Why then would I not offer the same courtesy to the leadership of the church that I expected from my staff—to be informed in advance? Such a practice would allow for questions to be raised and problems ironed out before presenting the proposal to the group.

In one church, where I was highly respected, I went to a meeting to decide about the hiring of a contractor for a new sound system. I had gathered all the information and met with the contactors myself. As I submitted my detailed proposal I was confident that the group would readily affirm my recommendation. After all, they liked me as a pastor and as a preacher. Furthermore, I had a strong recommendation to give them and I had more experience and knowledge in this matter

Leadership Mandates

than anyone else in the room. I already had taken two churches through this process and with great results. But when I came before them, I had done no advanced "spade work." I had not contacted the chair to share my recommendations or talked to any other members prior to sharing my well-documented presentation. I was unprepared for what happened next. It was the first "defeat" I had ever experienced at that church. The committee rejected my proposal and went with another contractor even though all the facts and recommendations were weighted heavily towards my recommendation. Why did this happen? As I look back on the event, I think one of the reasons it failed was that I had not properly informed the chair of my thinking on the matter. Perhaps the whole committee felt I had come to them only wanting them to quickly rubber stamp my recommendation. Perhaps I was so confident in my position I came off as condescending. Whatever the reason, their actions made me wonder if part of their vote was a rejection of my leadership in a rather secular decision—the choosing of a contractor. If I did not treat them with respect, perhaps they decided to withhold theirs from me.

Later in that same church, I again prepared to present a proposal to a committee. This time, however, I informed the chair in advance about what I was going to present and why I favored it. I did not ask for his support—I simply told him I wanted him to know this in advance, since he was the chair. To my surprise, after I had made my proposal the chair immediately offered his endorsement and the proposal was readily accepted. I was shocked with how easily it all went—not like the previous contractor decision. Ironically, this meeting was chaired by the same person who previously helped defeat my contractor proposal. Could the difference in outcomes have been the result of two different styles of leadership—one relying on "logic and the weight of the office" and the other based on true "joint decision making"?

Let me be clear. I do not offer the principle of "keeping the leadership informed" simply as a strategy for getting proposals approved, though that may be one benefit. I offer this policy of "staying connected" because it is how a pastor should treat the leadership—with respect and with a team approach. After many years of ministry I finally understood that I could keep my integrity, avoid playing politics and still share my plans with leadership in advance. It certainly does not hurt to have a few lay persons on one's side. Indeed, if I had cared then less about my false notion of "integrity" and more about securing important decisions for the church, I might have been "political" in the best sense of the word. This church helped teach me that I could actually keep my integrity and be a strong advocate at the same time.

I still believe in transparency. I refuse to work secretly behind the scenes to line up votes. But the chair of a committee has a right to know not only what items will come before the committee but to also have the privilege of the pastor's thinking before the meeting. Keeping such leadership informed is not only good strategy, good team planning; it is polite and considerate behavior. I recommend such practice for all pastors.

Leadership Mandates

Questions for Reflection

- Has an enemy ever been a source of insight for you?

- How could staying connected to those we don't like be a profitable thing to do?

- What is your strategy when coming before a committee with a proposal? How do you involve the leadership in the process? Do you also speak informally to committee members ahead of time?

- How would you define integrity in ministry? What actions must one avoid in order to maintain integrity? How important is integrity to you?

CHAPTER FIVE

SELF CARE ESSENTIALS

ACCEPT THE FACT THAT YOU WILL NEVER GET IT ALL DONE!

Try taking a day off. There will never be enough hours anyway.

It did not take me long to discover that the work load in ministry is an extremely heavy one. Whether one is an associate, a pastor of a small church, or the senior pastor of a large church there will always be tasks that need to be done that go unanswered. There is simply not enough time to do them all. I knew this is my head but I had never thought it through to its logical conclusion until my fourth church, a growing suburban church in a building program. I do not remember whether this crucial epiphany just came to me or if it was suggested by someone. The issue was taking time off. At that point in my ministry I usually took off most of Thursday but often had to come back to the church for an evening meeting. If I was behind in sermon preparation, I sometimes did a little work on the sermon during my day off as well. I soon realized I was not getting a true day off. My final conclusion was this: *I will never get all my work done whether I work seven days a week or six days a week, so why not take a full day off? The end result is the same!*

During this pastorate I made my first serious commitment to a complete day off. I asked the church to avoid any Thursday meetings that required my participation. I

Self-Care Essentials

informed the church of my regular day off so they would not expect to reach me unless for an emergency. For the remainder of my ministry I have stayed committed to a day off. I learned I needed it and that I was more efficient and healthier if I got it.

Having a day off did not mean for me a true Sabbath rest. I had errands to run and things to do around the house. But at least it gave me a break from ministerial responsibilities and that change of assignment was a welcome relief. A day off also meant the possibility of more family time and being able to be "present" with them when we were together rather than being so preoccupied I was there "in body only."

Several years earlier I had learned that it was important to designate a specific day off. I learned this prudent procedure when I had a "floating" day off in a smaller church. Someone asked me how many days off a week did I take? I was confused. "I take only one day off a week," I replied. The church member said he was confused because he had called for about three weeks in a row on different days and each day he called the secretary had said it was my day off! A regular day off also helps train the church members not to expect the pastor to be in the office, at the hospital or generally available on that day except for an emergency.

For those who have been in ministry for more than two years, I trust I do not have to make an argument for time off. Working too many hours will always catch up with the person—fatigue, illness, the loss of efficiency. But actually taking time off is difficult because there is always something that needs to be done, someone who needs to be visited, or something that needs some extra attention. The antidote for such a heavy sense of responsibility is to accept the fact that one person cannot do it all. I am reminded that even Jesus sometimes left the crowds, people with real needs to be met, and went off to be alone—to reflect, to meditate, to take a break. Even Jesus understood human limitations. There would always be someone he did not heal, someone he did not teach, and someone he did not reach. As pastors we will also have to leave undone some ministry that could have been accomplished.

Even after many years of practice in taking time away, I still have to be careful not to slip back into old habits. When there is much to be done in a church, I am always tempted to carve away some time from my day off or omit it altogether. If I do, I will pay the price through exhaustion or a minor illness and the time I usurped from a day off will be taken away by my time of recovery. The common saying is true for time away: "pay me now or pay me later." I vote for pay me now. I vote for a regular time off each week. It pays dividends not only to the pastor but also to the ones being served.

Self-Care Essentials

Questions for Reflection

- Do you take a regular day off that is protected from intrusions?

- Describe a typical day off. Is it normally enjoyable or is it just working hard at other tasks?

- Who, if anyone, has any claims upon your time off? Is a day off for your benefit alone?

- If you do not have a regular day off, what steps do you need to take personally and with the church to establish one?

- What day works best for a day off and why?

CARE FOR THE WHOLE SELF...MIND, BODY, AND SOUL!
It is not a matter of multiple choice!

Part of the responsibility of being a minister is taking care of the whole self—mind, body, and soul. Without such care we cannot do our best job because part of the self will be compromised. If we care for body and soul but neglect the mind, our ministry will lack the intellectual sharpness required by all our duties, especially that of communicating the gospel. If we take care of the mind and soul but neglect the care of the body, we are likely to be hampered by ill health and reduced life span. If we care for body and mind but fail to develop spiritual disciplines, then we will remain a spiritual lightweight, incapable of leading the flock in the deeper aspects of life. Our only option as ministers, if we are to be at our best, is to exercise great care in developing all three aspects—mind, body and soul.

It is hard to assess which of the three is most neglected by clergy in our present day. With obesity so prevalent not only in society but also among clergy, one could make the case for neglect of the body being a serious problem in ministry. Obesity's effect reaches far beyond the damage to the individual minister since it offers up a negative role model to members of the congregation. I remember in early ministry days when smoking and drinking were the designated no-no's for ministry. They were often treated more as mortal sins rather than simple sins against the body. One could now argue that drinking in moderation is many times less life-threatening than obesity. Care of the body must remain a base line for ministry rather than being seen as moral extra credit.

I would also argue, having listened to many preachers during my retirement years, that some in ministry have opted for "intellectual lite" in their preaching. I will confess than during my active ministry years I did not read enough quality material to stay as intellectually sharp as I would have liked. The temptation was often to "dummy down" sermons so all could understand them. That rationalization, however, is a cop out because a truly "intellectual" sermon can have great depth, yet still be understandable. Those of us in ministry must continue to grow intellectually, as well as keeping fit spiritually and physically. If not, we will have to be content that some of our congregation's limited biblical understanding will remain simplistic and unchallenged.

One might think that an area in ministry that few would neglect would be the spiritual side of life. Unfortunately, the pressures, distractions, and time restraints of ministry often make it difficult to deepen our own spiritual lives. We get practice in praying publically, but sometimes become spiritual amateurs in private. We may pray formally on behalf of others and then forget to pray for ourselves and for our own spiritual well-being. Spiritual health, however, remains an absolute essential to our ministry.

Most ministers have both a long suit and a short suit in regard to mind, body, and soul. Many of us are reasonably good at two out of the three. The challenge I am raising is that two out of three is not acceptable, that our short suits deserve some special attention because their neglect will be detrimental first to us and second to our congregation. Our members continue to look to us as an example of vitality and balance.

In other chapters I will explore the various steps one can take to develop these aspects of our lives. For now, I must simply insist the development of mind, body, and spirit is not a game of multiple choice. Like a good-running motor, we ministers must be hitting on all three cylinders or else settle for a rough and tenuous journey.

QUESTIONS FOR REFLECTION

- Do you agree that the health of mind, body, and spirit is essential for effective ministry?

- What is your short suit—the care of mind, body, or spirit? What have you done to shore up your weakest area? What clues or helps can others offer to get this area in shape?

- Who do you know that has been able to keep good health in each of the areas of mind, body and spirit? What is their secret?

Self-Care Essentials

DEVELOP SPIRITUAL DISCIPLINES!
Use prayer, study, sermon preparation, and moral living to grow spiritually.

In the last chapter I suggested that a minister needs to care for mind, body and spirit. None is more important than the care of the spirit. We are to be spiritual leaders even when we can seldom claim to be the most spiritually mature of our church. One of the greatest advantages of being a minister is that it almost forces us to grow spiritually. At least it forces us to be engaged in spiritual disciplines on a regular basis. I shudder to think what my spiritual quotient would be had I been in a secular profession. I don't know how I would have developed a discipline for Bible study and prayer.

In retirement, the spiritual discipline I miss the most is the benefit of weekly sermon preparation. First, there was the exposure to the Word and the concerted effort to make it applicable to daily living. I preached first to myself and second to the congregation, so preaching was always a place of discernment and an invitation to a more spiritual life. Second, nothing I have done in life has brought me closer to God on a regular basis than sermon preparation. I have always considered my sermon ideas to be the result both of my work and of God's inspiration. Preaching has been a partnership with God. Now that I do not preach on a regular basis I need to discover a new avenue for spiritual growth and an on-going partnership with God.

Prayer remains a growth area for me. I have always been one to pray on the go, to pray in the moment. I do not mean by that, praying in emergency only. I tend to pray in the midst of ordinary life and in short bursts of thought. Prayer at its best, I think, is a constant awareness of God's presence and God's will. It is the only way I can imagine Paul's notion of "praying without ceasing." My growth area is in structured praying. By that, I do not mean praying formally before others but in praying within the structure of a fixed time or place. Morning prayers or evening prayers offer a way to begin and end the day.

Study has certainly been a favorite means of spiritual growth for me. I am not implying that I am a scholar—far from it—but that Truth is of great importance to me. I could never settle on simply living out my faith; I must be able to both understand and communicate it. Study then becomes a major means of growth in my understanding of what the Truth is and how I am to live it. One of my regrets is that during full-time ministry I was not disciplined enough in reading. I did most of my heavy reading during vacation or during study leave, but rarely as an on-going discipline of weekly life.

I have chosen one avenue for spiritual growth that may seem surprising to some. I understand living a moral life as a means of growing spiritually. Many people see a moral life as an outgrowth of a strong inner spirituality—as if it is the crowning achievement. I, on the other hand, have found that as I have worked at being more moral in my behavior I have grown spiritually. By moral I do not mean refraining from doing wrong, but rather living a life of love. That life of love will manifest itself in certain principles like honesty and fidelity, but they are not ends in and of themselves, but rather a way of life that can become a part of us. For example, if I choose to be consistently honest day after day, there may come a time when honesty is a permanent part of me. I become an honest person, no longer having to *choose* to be honest, but only to engage a principle within me. I must be clear that such moral choosing does not make me "good," but simply allows me to gradually become closer to God by becoming closer to his will for creation.

Self-Care Essentials

One aspect of ministry that has helped me grow spiritually is the inescapable intimacy of the office. Ministers may choose to preach "fluff" but a minister's life is consumed with the most profound experiences of life—marriage, birth, baptism, sickness, tragedy, death, and grief. It is hard not to grow spiritually when one is exposed to God's Word on the one hand and the most poignant experiences of life on the other. Indeed, I credit the maturity of my present theology not to some superior reflective thought, but more to my experiencing the deep moments in the lives of parishioners while being immersed in the context of the Christian faith. As I have shown compassion to those experiencing tragedy, I have grown theologically and thus prepared myself for tragedy that would come into my own life. Ministry has enhanced my spiritual growth as I have walked through the valley and shadow of death with countless people under my care. I am grateful for being able to share the most poignant of human experiences and to witness the power of God at work in our midst.

Every minister will need to explore how he or she can best grow spiritually. Some choose a spiritual guide. Others go on spiritual retreats, while still others begin and end each day in a time of meditation and prayer. It matters not how we are able to maintain a healthy spiritual life, but only that we do so—not just for our sake, but also for the many who look to us for spiritual guidance.

QUESTIONS FOR REFLECTION

- What is the most helpful aspect of your spiritual life? How do you enhance that spiritual discipline?

- What is you greatest impediment to spiritual discipline? How might you overcome it?

- Is living a moral life a form of spiritual discipline? If so, how?

- Do you agree with the author that being with people in times of great need offers ministers a chance to grow spiritually and theologically?

Self-Care Essentials

WORK AT WORKING OUT!

Pay me now or pay me more later!

I am one of the fortunate ones—I know it. I don't love to just exercise, but I do love to compete. I have always been competitive and never more so than in the field of athletics. This means I have an advantage over many people—I love to exercise if I can do so while playing a competitive sport. I learned to play football when I was barely able to hold the ball. I have played football, basketball, and tennis—all with reckless abandon. For the past twenty-five years racquetball has been my game. All of these sports have helped me greatly in staying in shape and in keeping off the pounds that invariably appear around the half century mark, if not before.

There was only one time in my ministry when I almost gave up competitive sports. My wife and I had been discussing my time with family. My tennis, though I was playing only once or twice a week, did take place in the evenings when I could have been home with the wife and kids. For a time I gave up tennis and all other sports. I'm not sure if that resulted in more time with the family but at least I was not walking out the door, ready to have fun when the rest of the family were captive to the house and the doldrums. After a while though, I noticed that I was stressed out more than usual. I also was not feeling as good. After months with no competitive sports and little exercise, I made a decision for my own benefit. I would have to do something competitive. Perhaps this time I made concessions on when I played—I don't remember. What I do recall is that I made a conscious decision in my fourth appointment that I would never again voluntarily give up that part of my life.

Several years later my wife began to notice the difference in my behavior between times when I played sports and times when I did not. These non-active times were a result of illness or a heavy church work load or simply my failure to find a sports partner. To my complete surprise my wife said to me one day, "Why don't you go play tennis?" She had finally figured it out: I was in a better mood if I could have a regular outlet of competitive sports. From then on, I could sometimes conclude I was getting grumpy by my wife's emphatic suggestion to "go out and get some exercise."

If you could watch me play sports, you might wonder how it could be a stress reliever for me. I play with such intensity that one would be tempted to think it would increase stress, not diffuse it. I wondered about that myself for years, knowing that I played sports with more intensity than almost anything else I did. How could that be good for me? Of course, I knew there is a physical benefit of purging the body of poisons. There is the release of tension in the body as one totally exhausts oneself. But how could such physical intensity help me mentally except by increasing the flow of blood to the brain? One day someone finally explained it to me. "Justin, when you are on the court, what are you thinking about?" "Winning the next point," was my reply. "And what else are you thinking about?" "Absolutely nothing!" "There you have it!" he said with flair! He was right on target. Racquetball was a stress reliever because all those thoughts of church were pushed out of the way if only for the duration of a match. Life during the competition was extraordinarily simple: "Win the point, Justin!"

Through the years I have learned that competitive sports by themselves are often not enough to guarantee staying in shape. All great athletes know that physical training needs to be part of the mix. When my wife was ill with terminal cancer, I became physically exhausted. This was due in part to being the night care-giver and the subsequent sleep deprivation. But by working at church and being caregiver at home, I had no healthy outlet for my body. I decided that maybe exercise might help. I joined an athletic club and hired a personal trainer for three months. Unfortunately the trainer I picked turned out to be the seventh ranked featherweight boxer in the country. I soon feared that guy was going to kill me with exercise. There was one machine there that he loved and I hated. Occasionally it would be out of order. Perhaps once or twice in a lapse of spiritual maturity, I may have prayed that the machine would not be working. I did survive the machine, the trainer and the term of my contract. The training was indeed good for me. I found it helped me to be more resilient for my responsibilities at home and at work.

In my first church appointment after my wife died, I took on a new level of fitness training. I joined the local hospital's health facility and started training regularly with weights. It was then I learned that weight training can change one's metabolism. I did eat a bit more healthily but I did not put myself on a diet. Even so, in one year I lost 14 pounds. In addition, after measuring chest, arms, legs, and waist I discovered I had lost 14 inches total in all areas combined. I was almost sixty, but I was in the best shape of my life.

As I admitted from the start, I am the lucky one. I inherited a good metabolism, I love sports, and I don't mind working out. Consequently, I am in good health and staying in shape is much easier for me than for most people. But just because other people have a greater challenge with staying in shape does not give them a "get out of jail free" card. It is perhaps even more important for them to do whatever it takes to stay healthy: diet, exercise, weight training. The good news is that one does not have to be a great athlete in order to stay in shape. Walking is, in fact, a great way to exercise. Exercise machines are readily available for home and gym. Unless a medical condition prevents it, exercise for a healthy body is within reach for most people.

There is one final key to my being in shape at the present time: I eat less. True, I also eat more healthy foods. But the main reason I am not gaining weight presently is not so much *what* I eat but *how much*. When my wife and I eat out we most often split a meal. This is of course cheaper, but more importantly, it allows us to eat reasonable portions—not the size of a normal restaurant serving. Eating less, eating smarter, has made our lives healthier and in some ways a bit happier.

Each person must decide what plan works best. My suggestion is to have a partner for an exercise program—a friend, family member, or a professional trainer. (A word of caution: don't pick my former trainer!) Once you have started your regimen, stick to it. Don't quit. Your life may depend on it.

Questions for Reflection

- What is your biggest impediment to staying in shape?

- How healthy is your daily diet? What changes would improve it? Is portion size a factor?

- Is there an exercise program or sport that is both fun and effective? Is there an exercise program that is at least effective? Will you do it?

RECOGNIZE WHEN HELP IS NEEDED!
Call a counselor or ask for a minister!

In earlier chapters I mentioned times when I needed a counselor. In the first case I needed one but did not follow through. The result was several years of mild depression. I was not terribly unhappy. I was highly functional at work and reasonably functional at home. But I am convinced that if I had gone to a counselor during that time, I would have been a happier person and a more effective minister. In my crisis in ministry—one where a few strategized for my departure—I knew I needed help, at least with my anger. I went to the counselor and to my surprise I needed to work not only on the recent issue of the "ambush" but also on my resentment over how I was treated in a former church. Before I had finished with the counseling, I had resolved much of the residual resentment from these two different circumstances.

My next crisis did not come until nine years later. This time it would not be parishioners that would create the problem, but life itself. Two weeks after the tragedy of 9/11 my wife and I would experience our own catastrophe. My wife was diagnosed with terminal brain cancer. Our lives would be turned upside down until her death twenty-seven months later. Immediately after the diagnosis I realized that I would need help—and help on a regular basis. Unfortunately, many ministers foolishly think they are exempt from needing such support. But I knew if I were to get through the next few months or years, I would need not only support, but pastoral support. I also believed that it would be difficult for me to be both husband and minister to my wife. I called the two associates into my office and asked if they would be pastors for my wife and me. The younger associate agreed to make regular pastoral visits to my wife. He would be her pastor and would be

Self-Care Essentials

joined by the District Superintendent and later a Hospice Chaplain. For my clergy care I asked for the older associate who was not only steeped in the faith but one who had lost a spouse to cancer some ten years previously. What better guide could I have than one who had already journeyed through that dark valley?

Week after week I would visit with my pastor. We would always have prayer. She would always ask me how I was doing. For the first time I could fully understand how important pastoral care is to someone living through a tragedy. I am so thankful I was wise enough to know I would need help and so grateful to have such a wonderful guide for my journey.

There is a seductive notion that suggests that because we are shepherds we will never need a shepherd for ourselves. Do we not understand that we are sheep as much as our parishioners? We can choose to believe that as helpers, we should never need help. We can choose to believe such, but if so, we would be wrong. Even Jesus in the hour of his greatest need did not choose to experience Gethsemane by himself. He wanted and needed human comfort and support. We need no less.

We will not always be aware when we need help, but the people around us usually do. If someone suggests that we need help, it would be wise to accept their assessment. And what could it hurt to seek help? It could prove we are vulnerable—but we are. It could mean facing our anger and fears—but what better way to rid ourselves of them? Getting help could mean we could no longer stay in the comfort of self-pity or withdrawal. But it could also mean finding new joy and purpose. So when you realize you need help, look around and select someone you trust and give yourself a gift or two—gifts you have given to others—the gift of spiritual comfort and discernment. Take it from me, both are great gifts!

QUESTIONS FOR REFLECTION

- Have you ever needed help but failed to ask for it? If so, what price did you pay for not seeking help?

- When did you seek help and find it renewing or life-saving?

- As a minister do you ever need a minister? Give examples of times when having a minister would be helpful.

- Is going to a counselor a sign of weakness or an act of courage?

CHAPTER SIX

SHARPENING SKILLS AND STRATEGIES

TAKE TIME TO PLAN SERMONS LONG-TERM!
It improves the end result; it lessens the anxiety!

I have always believed in planning ahead. It is part of my nature. After I finish any meal I am always planning the next one. Of course, in preaching one has to a bit more long-term than that. By the time I was in my fourth church, I usually had about four sermons lined up at any one time. They were not fully developed—some had only a text, title and few main ideas. But at least I was not doing things week to week.

I remember clearly when I changed my practice in sermon planning. I wish I could say it was at my initiative, but it was not. My new planning regimen came as a result of a request from my new music director. "I need your sermon plans for the next seven weeks." "Why seven weeks?" I asked. "Because I want to plan the anthems to fit the sermons and I need to work on them with the choir for about seven weeks. Can you get me your sermon texts and titles soon?" I can't remember how quickly I responded to her request but before I left the church two years later, I had managed to complete six months of sermon plans at a time. To do this I spent part of my summer vacation doing the planning. Later I would ask the church not to count three of my vacation days as vacation, but instead as study leave.

Eventually I developed a yearly planning schedule. I would take off one week in January and plan the sermons for as much of the year as possible. Six months would be planned solidly and then additional sermon ideas would be listed but not linked to the calendar. In the summer, I would take about three days during my vacation to finish planning the rest of the year plus a few Sundays into the new year until my next January planning session.

My pattern for the planning retreat also became rather fixed. I would spend one day reading the lectionary texts for the entire year making notes about sermon ideas as I read. I interspersed time for reading, hikes, exercising, and meal preparation. I had a favorite place—a lake house offered to me by a parishioner. It was perfect because it was quiet and I knew no one in the area. I would cook my own simple meals, work for most of the day, watch the news, and do my planning. One day I would pick out the most developed sermon ideas and place them on the calendar. I began the practice of categorizing the sermons according to whether they focused on the Church, the Christian life, evangelism, exegesis, theology, the human condition, special days, or the liturgical seasons. Planning in advance helped me insure a balance in my preaching.

One church I served had no parsonage so my wife and I decided to build, a process that often lasts six months to a year. But we had a fantastic builder and he built the house, a wonderful house, in three months. How did he do it? He always tried to have five or six houses going at once but in different stages. When a framer finished with one house he would move to the next. When the painters were through with one house another one would be ready for them. He kept all his subs busy and he orchestrated the different stages of each house with great precision.

When I attended a preaching conference a year or so later, I decided to go to a workshop on long-range sermon planning. I was fascinated by the leader's analogy—building a house. He said to build a house takes time. You don't start one

Sharpening Skills and Strategies

week and finish it by the end of the week. You build it in stages. Building a sermon works the same way. When you are doing the finishing touches on one sermon you have the foundation ready for another. You move each sermon along until it is time to be delivered. That sounded a bit like my music director working on the anthem over weeks rather than attempting it after only one practice.

In doing my sermon planning, I often had sermon ideas that never made the cut for that year. I would carry them over to the next year's planning. Sometimes a sermon incubated for two years before I ever preached it. Some sermons develop quickly. Others really require time to be mulled over in our conscious and sub-conscious minds for a while. I have been known to move a sermon up on the schedule and move others back. Advanced planning allows sermons to reach their maturity before they are preached.

Long-term sermon planning was a gift initiated by a well-trained musician and then endorsed by countless seminars, conferences, and finally confirmed by practical experience. I only wish I had begun the practice in my first church instead of my fourth. Doing such planning has allowed me to see the broad strokes of my preaching and to be able to discern if my plan lacks balance or coherence. My advice is the same whether planning the next meal or crafting weekly sermons: Plan ahead!

QUESTIONS FOR REFLECTION

- How far ahead do you plan your sermons?

- What setting do you use for long-term sermon planning? What are your rituals and activities during your planning time?

- If you categorized one year's worth of sermons, what would be your list of categories and what would be the percentage for each category?

Sharpening Skills and Strategies

DARE TO PREACH WITHOUT A NET!
It keeps a strong connection between the preacher and the congregation!

Looking back on my ministry, I had three preaching styles: (1) preaching from extensive notes after doing a rough draft manuscript, (2) preaching from a "polished" manuscript and looking down as little as possible, and (3) preaching without notes (with a half sheet outline in my Bible). In each style the quality of the content was quite equal. The results were not equal, however. I can say with absolute certainty that preaching without notes has been by far the most effective method. Preaching from a completed manuscript was definitely the weakest of the three.

One danger of committing to a polished manuscript is that it becomes, in the process, more "literary" than "oral." There is more invested in saying things exactly as they are on the page—thus the need to look down to get it right. Sentences are often longer and more complex. Unfortunately, the polished manuscript form often sounds more like an essay than a conversation. During my "manuscript period" copies of my sermons were sent around the country and were well received. Regrettably, they were better "read" than "heard."

Preaching today, if it is to be effective, must have a *connection* between the preacher and the person in the pew. A conversational style is most effective. "Conversational" should not be mistaken for casual or off-the-cuff or without intensity. But the real energy should be between the preacher and the congregation, not the preacher and the manuscript. The listener wants to experience a person, not simply hear a sermon. Authenticity is of the essence.

How often have we been distracted as a poignant point is being made when the preacher glances down at the notes? It makes the preacher's words less believable even if the action is simply a nervous habit of a preacher afraid of not saying it perfectly. A preacher constantly bobbing up and down at the notes is like a dog lapping up water, trying with an occasional look upward to convince his owner that he cares more about him than the liquid contents of his bowl.

I must be quick to point out that the style I am presently promoting is not manuscript memorization—reciting what has been written. Nor is it an act of improv in sharing the Word. The general content has been carefully memorized, not as a precise script, but more like a sequence of stories. There is always room for ad lib—sometimes from the playfulness of the preacher's personality and sometimes from the prompting of the Holy Spirit. Throughout my ministry I have always believed that many of my sermon "insights" were more gifts of the Spirit than the creations of my own imagination. In the scary business of preaching without notes (or "preaching without a net"), one may well discover that the same Spirit that can speak to us in the study can also speak "live" in the very midst of the worship moment.

Whatever style one chooses in preaching, the energy—the connection—should always be between the preacher and the congregation. The "sermon" can never be *finished* on Thursday night or even Saturday night. A sermon must wait for its birth in the serendipity of the preached moment when its message is shared with the people. After all, a joke is not a joke until it is told. And a sermon, like a good joke, is not just a matter of what is said, but how one says it. Content, as important as it is, is only half the formula. Delivery is the place where words will either stay in stiff typed form or come to life through the authenticity of the preacher.

Sharpening Skills and Strategies

QUESTIONS FOR REFLECTION

- What is your preaching style? Do you use an outline? Do you use a manuscript?

- Are your sermons better read than heard?

- Who gives critical feedback to your sermons? How could that feedback be expanded?

- If you are not currently doing so, would you consider preaching without notes or with only one half sheet of paper?

BE A LEADER IN STEWARDSHIP!
Discover stewardship principles in your own life—then share them!

I wish I could say my commitment to tithing came after a deep spiritual awakening. Actually, the spiritual maturity came after making the commitment. It was my first annual conference as an ordained minister. I was newly married and our combined income as preacher and teacher was far short of affluence—we were scraping by. During the first day, in the midst of the usual debate over the conference budget, a minister rose to make a motion. "I move that the ministers of the North Texas Annual Conference all pledge to tithe their salary for this conference year." To easily count the vote, the chair asked that all who favored the motion stand. To be honest, I stood more to avoid embarrassment than as a gracious act of giving for the work of the church. I did, however, have one conscious fear as I stood to be counted: I would have to explain my actions to my bride of two years. I did not look forward to that task.

When I arrived home that evening I offered my best persuasive argument to my wife for my decision and then waited for her response—which came only after what seemed like a very long and reflective pause. (I did not know if the time lapse was a good sign or only a prelude to real trouble.) When she finally responded, she spoke emphatically: "I think I'll tithe my salary also." And that was that. We had just increased our giving to the church by about three times. It was a decision I never regretted. I learned from that experience that one does not have to be deeply moved to commit to tithing. All that is really required is to do it. The meaning and joy of tithing often come later.

Throughout my ministry I have been a strong advocate of stewardship. I have always felt stewardship was firmly grounded in both scripture and theology. We do not own all

Sharpening Skills and Strategies

that we have; we are only stewards. Because of this understanding we are encouraged to share what we have with the needs around us and with the church whose life and work we value immensely. Good stewardship is both a sign of spiritual maturity and a means toward obtaining it.

In all my churches I have made certain that we have a yearly stewardship emphasis. I never like to call it a stewardship "campaign" since that sounds so commercial and can lead to the false notion that stewardship is only about money. It really is about all the gifts we share, including our talents. One year I was shocked to learn that in a very large church I was serving there were no plans to have a stewardship program except to receive pledges on pledge Sunday. The reason the leaders offered was that no one would volunteer to head the committee. I tried my best to sell the importance of a full-scale emphasis but the committee was not budging—there would be no program that year. "What if I volunteered to do it?" I asked, as if I had nothing to do with my time. The committee agreed that I could head the committee. It was then that I offered one condition to my leadership: the church would send me to a stewardship seminar. The committee agreed.

Fortunately, I found a course offered on stewardship and immediately enrolled. It was taught by a pastor of a large church and he laid out a step-by-step plan including a list of all the committees, detailed job assignments and a six-month time-line. I have used part or all of his general planning in almost every church since then. But the surprise of the seminar came when he suggested that the pastor not only set an example by giving generously to the church, but also that such stewardship be communicated to the church in some way—through personal witness, pastoral reflection, or a letter to the congregation. The bottom line was that the pastor needed to share a personal stewardship story to the entire congregation. Such a witness should not be for the purpose of self-aggrandizement but only as an incentive for the congregation to follow the lead of the clergy.

I decided to use the detailed stewardship plan in my church, including the part of a personal stewardship witness. I asked all Sunday school classes to meet in the sanctuary during the allotted hour and there shared with them my own circuitous journey of stewardship, primarily focusing on the financial support of the church. I began by telling them how I started tithing and the meaning it had to me through the years. In addition to my witness on that day, the over-all program also included lay people sharing their stories about what the church had meant to them and the role that giving had played in their own spiritual journey.

At the end of the stewardship program the church enjoyed a significant increase in both pledges and weekly giving. From that day forward, I made it a point to give sacrificially to the church and to occasionally make that known to the congregation, not for bragging rights, but to assure them I was a true partner in supporting the life and work of the church. Other ministers may choose to keep giving private, a practice I had for most of my ministry, but, even so, I trust such giving will still be exemplary.

Stewardship, of course, cannot be implemented simply through an annual program but must be an integral part of the church's life. In the financial aspect of stewardship I have adopted several principles to enhance the financial workings of the church. Listed below are a few of my strategies to improve the financial health of the church.

- ❖ Fill the Finance Committee with people who give generously instead of stacking it with accountants and finance professionals. Finance members should be "big picture" rather than "bottom line" people.

Sharpening Skills and Strategies

- ❖ Convince the Finance Committee that their job is not to hold the purse strings of the church's spending but rather to insure that the financial needs of the church are undergirded by the congregation. Their job is to be governed more by what the church truly needs than to simply spend what has been given.
- ❖ If the church is healthy, if the financial goal is realistic, if the church is kept informed of this need throughout the year, then the church will most often be able to reach that goal or come very close to it.
- ❖ Never borrow from designated funds except in an extreme emergency and only then if it is done with transparency and a full commitment to repay it as soon as possible.
- ❖ If designated funds have been usurped by the finance committee in the past, work to rightfully repay them. Without such integrity people will be slow to give to specific needs fearing that those funds will go elsewhere.
- ❖ Preach on the importance of giving without apology. The level of giving, just as the level of service, is an indicator of commitment to the church. Great service is not a replacement for giving nor is giving a proxy for service. Both are needed and required.
- ❖ Financial stability should never be at the cost of mission. To do so is to suggest that our purpose is institutional survival rather than ministry beyond ourselves.
- ❖ A church will find it difficult to be in mission if it is constantly wrestling with the issue of financial survival. Helping the church find a realistic financial goal and then underwriting it is a major responsibility of a pastor. Through creativity, example, and wise strategy a pastor can lead the congregation into financial stability and thus free it to do its work of mission and ministry.

QUESTIONS FOR REFLECTION

- Would you be ashamed or embarrassed if the church knew your level of giving?

- What role have you played in helping the church grow in its total stewardship? What steps can you take to improve your leadership in this area?

- If you do not have much training or experience in stewardship matters, are you willing to commit to such training in the near future?

Sharpening Skills and Strategies

ADOPT A LESS-ANXIOUS PRESENCE!
It will be a blessing to you while having a calming effect on the church.

I am relieved that the phrase "non-anxious" presence, prevalent in systems theory literature, has been re-named by some as "less-anxious" presence. Both of these phrases are often found in the training materials for interim ministers. As a recovering Type A personality, I knew early on that a "non-anxious" presence would be impossible for me. A "less-anxious" presence, as a relative term, just might be within my reach.

I have come to deeply appreciate the term "less-anxious presence" after having practiced it almost instinctively during my first interim appointment. I had been exposed to the term "less-anxious presence" prior to that appointment but it had never been fully consummated through my pastoral experience. The appointment itself had all the makings of an immense anxiety producer. A beloved senior pastor had died tragically at the age of fifty leaving a grieving family and a devastated church. I entered an atmosphere of deep grief and high anxiety. Many even worried about the future of the church since it had been heavily invested in its dynamic and charismatic pastor. When I first met the leadership of the church, they seemed committed not so much on eliminating my fears, as in making certain I knew the seriousness of their situation, including an imploding financial crisis.

What I learned from this experience, so fraught with anxiety, is that my faith and personal experiences were of far more consequence in determining my "presence" than my psychological profile. Indeed, it was my faith and life journey that made me confident that this church would not only survive, but also thrive once again. Had I not believed this, and believed it strongly, I would not have been able to exude a "less-anxious" presence to those gathered at the first meeting and later to those attending the first worship service.

It was in fact my life story that was the main reason I accepted this challenging appointment only two years after retiring from active ministry. I felt that my personal life experience gave me tremendous insight into the struggles that this congregation and staff had experienced as they had witnessed the illness and death of such a beloved pastor. My own story had many parallels to theirs. Some seven years earlier my first wife had been diagnosed with a malignant brain tumor. She lived for twenty-seven months and was active in the church until the last five months of her life. I served as the senior pastor throughout that time. Both churches had been blessed by the witness of a life well-lived, even in the midst of tragic illness and an early death.

As the new interim senior pastor I knew all too well the emotional strain the church experienced by observing such a prolonged illness, even in spite of the positive effect of such an exemplary witness. In addition, there would be many engaged in intense theological wrestling as they were confronted with what seemed to be "unjust" suffering. It was extremely difficult for these two congregations, mine and theirs, to witness the devastating effects of a terminal illness followed by the inevitability of death. In the case of the present church, the pastor who had ministered so well to them was now gone. They felt like sheep without a shepherd.

Yet I had a distinct advantage of perspective over this grieving congregation. They were in the very throes of grief. I had already undergone immense healing from my previous loss. Even though I intensely felt their grief, I did so knowing that there was indeed hope for their healing as well. I was convinced that healing would come to them, not through the passing of time, but through the faith they held dear, the comforting embrace of their spiritual community, and the workings of the Spirit. In the midst of the church's turmoil, I could exhibit a "less-anxious" presence. Even though I experienced their deep emotion, I was constantly undergirded with an assurance that God's grace would not only heal their individual grief, but also plant the church on a firm foundation for its future.

I discovered in that first interim appointment that my assurance of their healing was enhanced by my compassion for them. I not only knew that they would be better; I also felt empathy, remembering vividly what it was like to lose someone so close. As one who understood what they were experiencing, my presence was rightly interpreted as a gift of deep empathy. Yet, as often the case with pastoral concern, the compassion shown becomes symbolic of God's ultimate concern as well.

The "less-anxious" presence that I was able to give came not only from my compassion and empathy for the congregation, not only from my faith in God's power, but also from my strong belief in God's own compassion, a non-anxious presence beyond our knowing. My theology of God's presence, coupled with human compassion, had a specific text. The words are from Paul in his second letter to the church at Corinth:

> Blessed be the God and Father of our Lord Jesus Christ, the Father of mercies and the God of all consolation, who consoles us in all our affliction, so that we may be able to console those who are in any affliction with the consolation with which we ourselves are consoled by God.
> (2 Corinthians 1:3-4)

The role of the pastor coming into an anxious system, whether one of division, grief, or disillusionment, is to reflect a positive spirit, one grounded not in denial or wishful thinking, but in the power of God to transform both individuals and community. Ultimately, it is the pastor's own faith that makes possible a "less-anxious" presence in the midst of deep emotion and tragic circumstances. Without such faith and theological integrity, a pastor, no matter how psychologically mature, will not be able to bring a calming presence to a hurting congregation. But equipped with such faith, a pastor can well bring a source of healing and calm.

Sharpening Skills and Strategies

QUESTIONS FOR REFLECTION

- Have you ever exhibited a "less-anxious" presence in the face of a very emotionally charged situation? If so, how were you able to exhibit such a presence?

- Have you ever witnessed someone bringing calm to a very anxious group of people? What did you observe happening in that situation?

- What role do you think faith could play in empowering one to have a less-anxious presence?

CHAPTER SEVEN

RESPONDING TO GOD'S CALL

LOOKING BACK WITH THANKS!
Ministry, even in the tough times, has great potential for joy!

The main purpose for writing this book is to share my insights into the practice of ministry in the hope that what I have learned on my journey will be helpful to those presently engaged in pastoral ministry. If the reader can glean valuable insights from my experiences and thereby avoid some of the pitfalls I have encountered, then my efforts are sufficiently rewarded. It is my further hope that present-day clergy will be able to put these principles and insights into practice far earlier in their ministry than I was able to do. I wish I had known in the beginning what I know now. If so, I would have been a more effective minister and probably a happier one.

Writing this book has also given me an opportunity to carefully reflect over thirty-eight years of ministry, pondering both its pains and its joys. In retrospect, being a minister has always been meaningful work even when times were tough. Never in all those years did I ever question whether or not God had called me into ministry. On a few occasions, however, I did question whether or not I wanted to continue living out that call. The title of the book suggests that dichotomy: "*Surviving and Thriving in Ministry.*" Looking back, I have concluded that for most of my ministry, I did far more than survive. At times I

Responding to God's Call

even thrived in my life's calling. Even so, there were also those dark nights of the soul where survival was the order of the day.

It is my firm belief that being a minister is a most difficult profession, loaded with challenges, stress, and an enormous amount of vulnerability. The high exit rate of clergy is in part a direct result of its many pressures, temptations, and pitfalls. But as I contemplate my years in ministry, I am inclined to think that I often focused too much on the difficulties, irritations, and stress of ministry and too little on its countless privileges. Though ministry remains one of the more difficult of pursuits, we clergy should remind ourselves that other professions have similar downsides. For example, ministry is vulnerable to criticism, but so is public office. Ministers are sometimes underpaid, but not as much as public school teachers. Ministry is stressful, but not nearly as much as that sustained by our present-day military. Ministers are misunderstood, falsely accused, and wrongfully judged but where is there escape from any of these difficulties? Everyone suffers injustices. I must confess that on rare occasions I felt devalued as a minister when I was, in fact, gratefully received and deeply appreciated by most of my flock. The problem was that I gave too much credence to the negative voices of a few allowing them to temporarily drown out the affirmations and support of so many. My mistake.

Having argued that ministry is a most stressful and vulnerable profession, it is only fair to acknowledge some of its benefits. To do so, suggests that ministry is as much a sacred privilege as it is a heavily-laden responsibility. To its credit, ministry is irrevocably centered in things that truly matter in life—values, community, human compassion, the spiritual realm, the immeasurable gift of forgiveness. Of course, one still has to maneuver through the mundane and trivial, but these are inconsequential when one is intimately involved in a ministry to people in need of grace. Ministry can and does thrive when our efforts, coupled with the Spirit of God, make a difference—a positive difference—in the lives of people.

I can recall several key times when my ministry thrived. Ironically, this often occurred following a time of trial. If I learned from my mistakes and did not become bitter from them, then I had an opportunity to grow as a person and as a pastor. It has been the mistakes, not the successes that have nudged me to re-invent myself time after time. It has been the valleys, not the mountain tops that have deepened my empathy and heightened my resolve. After years of service, I have become a stronger leader and a more secure person, and consequently have experienced of late an even more joyful and rewarding ministry. Knowing what I now know about ministry, its challenges and its rewards, I would still do it all over again. If I were asked today to respond to God's call, to start again from the very beginning, I would still rise to say, "Here am I; send me!" (Isaiah 6:8) But in another sense God's call has never left me. I am, you see, *minister for life*—and that, my friends, is good news—good news indeed!

Responding to God's Call

QUESTIONS FOR REFLECTION

- What insights into ministry have you discovered in reading this book? Have you put any of these into practice?

- How difficult is it to be a minister? What is the hardest part of the job or of the experience of being in ministry?

- Are you a minister for life? If so, is this realization encouraging or depressing?

- How is one fortunate to be a minister? What are its built-in joys?

SURVIVING OR THRIVING?

It has little to do with circumstance and everything to do with faith and love!

After carefully reflecting on thirty-eight years of ministry, I now view it more as gift and less as an awesome responsibility. To be sure, throughout my ministry I have been extremely conscientious in my work, always being aware of its importance. I am now convinced, however, that working harder will not make ministry more enjoyable or even more efficient. Working smarter, working always with the big picture in mind, working without our hearts on our sleeves—these approaches will indeed produce a more effective and happier clergy.

Of one thing I am certain, we will never flourish as ministers if we insist on carrying with us the irritations, hurts, and injustices that befall us. There have been many Christian martyrs in the distant past as well as in the present, but our occasional suffering at the hand of others will not be enough to nominate us for sainthood. Best we let go of our resentments, stop dressing our wounds, and simply immerse ourselves in the task of serving.

Like churches, ministers do not do well staying in the survival mode. We pastors will all encounter difficulties but we should never allow them to permanently ensnare us or defeat us. We were intended to thrive—not merely survive. Part of the success of our thriving and surviving depends on how well we learn from our mistakes. This learning includes recognizing our folly, admitting it, and then avoiding those erroneous ways in the future.

The term I like to use for growing professionally as well as personally is *re-inventing oneself.* This transformation is rarely comprehensive; we do not show improvement in every aspect all at once. Rather, we whittle away at some action, some habit,

Responding to God's Call

some attitude that is proving counter-productive, and then we commit to changing it, purging it from our day-to-day behavior. We *re-invent* ourselves, little by little, piece by piece, until the whole has a new and more attractive appearance. None of this desired improvement is simply self-administered; it comes about only by the grace of the One who has called us.

My hope for the clergy of today is that they will not allow the pettiness and meanness of people to detract them from the purpose and work of ministry. My further hope is that they will be secure enough in themselves, in the power of the faith, and in the importance of their work that that they will be somewhat immune to the sting of unfair criticism, never allowing negativity to break their spirits or dampen their joy.

As I prepare to rest my case for the richness of a life in ministry, I have high hopes that some of the insights I have shared will help make ministry less a responsibility to be duly executed, and more a life to be immensely enjoyed. If Christ wanted abundant living for us all, surely he wants abundant ministry for all who answer God's call. On this day I want no less for all clergy.

It is not enough that we *survive*. We are meant to *thrive*. So may it be!

QUESTIONS FOR REFLECTION

- Are you thriving in ministry? If not, why are you not doing so? What would need to change for your ministry to be more than simply survival?

- How long has it been since you have re-invented yourself? What would be your first area to improve?

- Do you ever practice ministry as though you are a Christian martyr instead of a servant of the Lord?

- Are you ready to thrive in ministry? What steps must you take to begin?

Made in the USA
Charleston, SC
18 August 2014